A Garland Series

The English Stage
Attack and Defense 1577 - 1730

A collection of 90 important works
reprinted in photo-facsimile in 50 volumes

edited by
Arthur Freeman
Boston University

A Defence of Plays

by

Edward Filmer

with a preface
for the Garland Edition by

Arthur Freeman

Garland Publishing, Inc., New York & London

1972

Copyright © 1972

by Garland Publishing, Inc.

All Rights Reserved

Library of Congress Cataloging in Publication Data

Filmer, Edward, fl. 1707.
   A defence of plays.

   (The English stage: attack and defense, 1577-1730)
   Reprint of the 1707 ed.
   1. Collier, Jeremy, 1650-1726. A short view of the
immorality and profaneness of the English stage.
3. Theater--Moral and religious aspects. 3. Theater--
England. I. Title. II. Series.
PN2047.C62F5 1972   792'.013   70-170449
ISBN 0-8240-0619-4

Printed in the United States of America

Preface

Born about 1651, probably at Westminster, Edward Filmer matriculated at Corpus Christi in 1668, held a fellowship at All Soul's (B.A. 1672), and was a lawyer (B.C.L. 1676 and D.C.L. 1681, at Gray's Inn by 1675, when his father is termed a baronet) before attempting a play. In 1697 he published "a lugubrious blank verse tragedy of extreme length" [Gordon Goodwin], The Unnatural Brother, *and in 1707 brought forth this sensible if tardy response to Jeremy Collier's* Short View. *Collier replied to it briefly with* A Farther Vindication *in 1708.*

A Defence of Plays *is reprinted from a copy of the original edition in the possession of the Publishers. It collates A-$L^8 M^4$ ($M4^v$ blank), lacking [A1] (half-title, which has been supplied from a copy at Yale [Ik V275 T698]).*

Lowe-Arnott-Robinson 339.

July, 1972   A. F.

5

FILMER's

DEFENCE

OF

PLAYS.

A

DEFENCE

O F

PLAYS:

O R,

The Stage vindicated,

From several Passages in

Mr. *Collier*'s *Short View*, &c.

Wherein is offer'd

The most Probable Method of Reform-
ing our PLAYS.

With a Consideration

How far Vicious Characters may be allow'd
on the STAGE.

By *Edward Filmer*, Doctor of the Civil Laws.

LONDON: Printed for *Jacob Tonson*, within *Grays-Inn* Gate, next *Grays-Inn* Lane. 1707.

THE
PREFACE
TO THE
READER.

MY *Concern to see the Stage so vi-olently affaulted on the one hand, and so strangely deferted on the* other, was that which first tempted me *to engage in the Defence of a Diversion, which I always thought might be so ma-naged, as to be not only innocent but ufe-ful.*

It is true indeed that many great Abu-ses have of late Years taken, as it were, Poffeffion of our Stage; and it is as true, that Mr. Collier *has greedily enough fnapt at that Opportunity of blackening and rendring it as odious as may be, of cenfu-ring our Poets, and reprefenting them as the Promoters of Vice, and Incouragers of Debauchery. Nay, without afcribing*

any

any thing to the Rashness and Inadvertency of Youth, to the Incouragement and Example of a vicious Age, or the more prevailing Hopes of some worldly Advantage, (either of which Motives, tho' criminal enough, might yet with greater Probability, and more Charity, have been urg'd as the unhappy Occasion of their Errors) he boldly encroaches on the Prerogative of the Almighty, he pretends to dive into the very deepest Secrets of their Hearts, and roundly tells us their Design was to discountenance Religion, and propagate Atheism As for their Intentions, they are plac'd out of my Reach, and therefore I shall not presume to meddle with them, neither is it my Design either to defend or excuse any of those their real Faults, which in my Opinion would be better and much easier mended than defended. On the contrary, my Meaning is so far only to vindicate the Stage, as it may be clear'd from all that Lumber, reform'd from all those Abuses, which have made such a Noise in the World, and oblig'd Mr. Collier with so very fair an Opportunity of exposing our Poets as Atheists, and representing the Stage as a Place hated by God, and haunted by the Devil.

For

The PREFACE.

For my part, I am as much for a fair and reasonable Reformation of the Stage, as Mr. Collier himself can pretend to be, how much soever I may differ from him in the Means requisite to so desirable an End. And I am apt to believe, that the soft and gentle Interposition of a profess'd Friend, may operate more effectually on the generous Nature of our Poets in order to it, than all the Wit, all the quaint Flourishes or satyrical Lashes of an imbitter'd Enemy; which Opinion it was that, at last, turn'd the Scale, and prevail'd with me to venture this little Piece into the World; where it had appear'd without so much as the common Ornament of a Preface, but that I thought it almost necessary to obviate some Objections which might be rais'd against it by the Curious, and explain some Passages which might seem any way obnoxious to the Misconstruction of the scrupulous Reader.

When Mr. Collier's Short View first appear'd abroad, many of our Poets took the Alarm; but it was only in order to secure themselves. For whilst every one flew to the Defence of his own particular Concern, the Stage was left naked, exposed to all the most furious Assaults of a violent and implacable Enemy: Or if by chance any one appear'd early in the Breach,

A 4   'twas

twas only to defend the Stage with all its *Abuses*, without any the least *Regard* to such a convenient and due *Regulation* of it, as has been expected, and for a considerable time earnestly desir'd by the most sober and unprejudic'd Part of the *Nation*. In the mean time above two *Years* slipt away, whilst they were still washing the *Blackamore*, and I still wavering, still in hopes that somebody of greater *Abilities* than my self, would at last attempt something in order to the *Reformation*, as well as the *Defence* of the *Stage*. But after so long an *Expectation*, nothing of that nature appearing, I thought it high time, if at all, to set my *Hand*, how feeble soever, to the *Work*. And this is the Reason why this *Piece* appears so late in the *World*.

But there are some, I doubt not, who at the very first *Sight* of these few *Sheets*, will be apt to cry out, *Why all this Noise, all this Stir about Plays? Why this eternal Wrangling about a Matter of meer Diversion only?* Be it so: Yet I tell thee, *Reader*, many great and unexpected *Events* do frequently flow from very slight and trivial *Beginnings*. We, or our *Fathers*, have seen *Three* flourishing *Kingdoms* brought to the very *Brink* of *Ruin*, a great, good and pious *King* murder'd on a Scaffold, Three Young Princes shamefully chas'd from their own Native Country, and all by the unnatural Violence of some hot-headed Zealots, who ran their first Heat indeed against Lawful Sports after Evening Service on Sundays, against Wakes, Feasts, Garlands and Maypoles on Holy-Days, and other such like innocent Diversions of the Vulgar; but never stopp'd in their Career, 'till in Contempt of all Laws, both Divine and Human, they had utterly, and as they thought irrecoverably, overthrown both Church and State.

I do not pretend to tax our Modern Writers against the Stage, with any such pernicious and wicked Design; much less Mr. Collier, who is, I am well assur'd, a Gentleman of very different Principles from those of our unhappy Reformers. I only wish he had consider'd a little better, before he had so positively declar'd all Plays condemn'd by the Holy Scripture; since he cannot but know what Use some bad Men have formerly made of that Holy Writ, how miserably soever wrested from its true and genuine Sense; and every Child can tell us, that he that puts a Sword into a Mad-man's Hand, will be thought accessary, at least, to all the Mischief he does with it. Mr. Collier has

in-

The PREFACE.

indeed, whether designedly or not I shall
not pretend to determine, very much oblig'd a certain Sort of People who are, I
doubt, as great Enemies to our Church as
to our Stage, and who wou'd, cou'd they
with Impunity do it, quickly make as
great an Outcry against the one as the o-
ther; he has dress'd up all their old Cant
against Plays, in a new, gay and fashionable Garb; in a word, he has attack'd
us with the only Weapon they never yet
knew the Use of, I mean, Wit. Take a-
way that, and you will see nothing in
that celebrated Piece of his, but what
has been before urg'd above a hundred
times, and as often answer'd. Nothing
(except what he presses against some particular Abuses, which we desire may be
reform'd as much as he can do) but what
strikes equally at all other the most innocent Recreations whatsoever: And I do
not at all question, but that had those
strait-lac'd Gentlemen, with Mr. Collier's
charitable Assistance, once gain'd their
Point against Plays, we should quickly
find them nibbling at most of our other
Diversions, and giving our Ladies as
frightful an Idea, perhaps, of Hidepark
or the Mall, as Mr. Collier has already
done of the Play-house. Then, a Round
or two in the one should certainly be attended

The PREFACE.

tended with some Appearance, at least, of Evil; and an Evening's Walk in the other infallibly be censur'd as one of those scandalous and unfruitful Works of Darkness, from which St. Paul so earnestly dissuades us. Nor indeed does Mr. Collier himself so much discountenance those severer Methods of proceeding as he might have done, tho' somewhere in his View, I must confess, he does tell us, that he has nothing to say against innocent Recreations. For that methinks, at the best, is but a very cold sort of an Expression, and seems to intimate thus much, at least, that as he has nothing to say against them, so has he but very little, or nothing at all, it may be, to say for them. But I shall urge this no farther, what I have already said being enough to convince all reasonable and unprejudic'd Persons, of the Importance of this Dispute about Plays; and let 'em plainly see, that granting them to be a matter of meer Diversion only, (from which Aspersion however Mr. Collier himself takes great Pains to clear them) yet is not the Controversie of so very slight and trivial a Nature as some People would have it thought: Since in vindicating the Use of a Reform'd Stage, we at the same time assert that of our Christian Liberty, which allows us a

rea-

reasonable and moderate Enjoyment of the innocent Pleasures of this World: Nor indeed can we yeild up the one, without betraying the other to the pretended Zeal of ev'ry designing Hypocrite.

There are two sorts of Persons, that may perhaps severely enough censure this my Attempt in favour of the Stage.

To the first however, consisting of such as from their very Infancy, perhaps, may have been taught to look upon all Plays as utterly unlawful and damnable, I shall say no more but this, that I cannot imagine upon what reasonable Grounds, any one can think that Diversion damnable, which 'till of late Years has been allow'd in all Christian Kingdoms and Nations in the World; which is no where censur'd in the Holy Scripture, nor has ever yet been plainly and formally condemn'd by any one Council, or legal Assembly of Christian Bishops whatsoever.

As for the second sort of Persons, consisting of such as think Plays lawful, but yet are offended at those Liberties many of our Modern Poets have pretended to in their Dramatick Compositions, and may possibly be dissatisfy'd at the Latitude by me allow'd in the Use of vicious Characters, any otherwise than as they may serve, not only as Foils to
                                        heighten

heighten and set off those Characters of Virtue, design'd by the Poet for Imitation, but as a charitable Sea-Mark too, to shew and point at those fatal Rocks on which all those are sure at last to dash, that dare still steer on in that or the like dangerous Course of Vice. And this, I think, may be enough to justifie the Use of Vicious Characters in general; yet in particular, I doubt, I may be blam'd still by some, for what I have said on the Subject of Swearing, and represented as a Favourer of that Vice, whilst on any Terms I seem to allow the Character of a common Swearer a Place on the Stage. Now to this, tho' I need say no more, than that the very same thing may be objected against me, in the Case of all other Vices as well as this; yet Swearing being a Sin generally very hateful to all, and to some, I doubt not, therefore only the more odious because unprofitable, I desire the Reader to take notice, that I do no where recommend the Use of it to our Poets. No, I very well know there never was, nor ever will be any such Character brought on the Stage. For besides that Swearing in it self is but a dull, heavy Vice; there must necessarily enter more of it into the compleat Composition

of

The PREFACE.

of an habitual Swearer than can be consistent with those Limitations, propos'd as necessary in the Case of all Vicious Characters; and this consequently must fall foul on that great and general Rule of common Decency, at all times religiously to be observ'd on the Stage, unless on very extraordinary Occasions.

Having said thus much in Answer to several, as I conceive, the most material Objections, that may probably be raised against this [Piece, I shall now speak but a Word or two to one more, which may in general be argued against this,] or any other Attempt of the like Nature, viz. That it may encourage some People to spend too much time in the Play-house.

In answer to which, I can only say and protest to the Reader, that 'tis no part of my Design so to do; nay, I should think my self extreamly unhappy, if on the account of any thing I have said any Person whatsoever should be tempted to borrow but one single Minute more from his Business or his Devotion, than what he would otherwise have done. All I pretend to is, that the same reasonable Proportion of Time, which any one in his own Conscience shall be persuaded he may innocently spare from either, may as well be

spent

The PREFACE.

spent in the seeing of a well regulated
Play, as in any other Recreation whatsoever ; nay on this one Account much
better, because the one can at the best
but Divert, and the other may at the
same time both Divert and Instruct him
too.

And now, Reader, I willingly deliver
up this little Piece to the Mercy of the
Zealot on the one hand, and the Critick
on the other. If either of them, dislik-
ing what I have offer'd, shall think fit to
propose any other practicable Method tending either to a fairer, or stricter Regulation of the Stage, I shall be one of the first
to Applaud so good and commendable a
Design. For however this my weak Attempt may be censur'd, yet, I do assure
thee, 'twas well meant ; and that I do
not pretend to plead for any thing, but
what in my Conscience, and according to
the best of my Judgment, I think may be
very safely and innocently admitted. All
that I apprehend is, that Censure which
may justly enough be pass'd on the Meanness
of the Performance, and yet even in that
Case I have this Consolation left, that the
Justice of the Cause may, perhaps, shine
the brighter through my Weakness. But
to confess the Truth, whatever the Success

The PREFACE.

cefs may be, I shall not be over-much concern'd at it ; for as, were I never so able, I
would not willingly offer to maintain a
bad Caufe ; so neither shall I be very folli-
citous, tho' through any Infirmity of mine,
I should happen to mifcarry in the Defence
of a good one.

A DEFENCE OF PLAYS,

(As they may and ought to be Reform'd)

Againſt the

Underhand Attack

OF

Mr. *COLLIER*, &c.

IT is now a conſiderable Time, ſince Mr. *Collier* firſt publiſh'd his *View of the Immorality and Prophaneſs of the* Engliſh *Stage:* A Piece! that has been receiv'd by the World with a general Applauſe, and ſtood the Shock of ſome of

B   the

the greateſt Wits of the Age: A Piece! that together with the ſpecious Title of Reformation, ſeems to carry its Protecti- on too in its Front; as pretending to no- thing more than a free, and juſt Cenſure of thoſe many and great Abuſes which have, of late Years, crept in upon our *Engliſh* Stage. This is indeed a very plauſible Pretence, and not to be oppos'd without manifeſt Danger to the Oppo- nent; eſpecially when manag'd by a Man of Mr. *Collier's* Abilities, who is certain- ly a Perſon of great Parts, and good Learning. But notwithſtanding theſe, and ſome other Reaſons, which might very well have diſſuaded, if not wholly diſcourag'd me from interpoſing in this Diſpute; yet Truth alone out-weighing them all, in Purſuit of that, I ſhall now at length venture to enquire a little far- ther into the Merits of the Cauſe; and take the Liberty of examining ſomething nearer into the Deſign of that Book, than any of thoſe Gentlemen, I think, have yet done, who have hitherto pretended to oppoſe it. Not that I am ſo vain as to imagine, that I can have made any o- ther Diſcoveries, than what any one elſe might have done as well, or indeed much better than my ſelf: But the Miſchief of it *is,* thoſe Gentlemen that are moſt able, and

and moſt concern'd, to give a Check to Mr. *Collier*'s Deſign upon the Stage, ſeem ſtill more eager to defend their own Faults, than either willing or forward to take Notice of his.

Had Mr. *Collier* appear'd only as a Reformer of our Plays, all the World, I think, muſt have applauded ſo good, ſo bold, ſo generous a Deſign. But he, under the Pretence of Reforming, Undermines the Play-houſe; and with its Abuſes, endeavours to take away the Thing too. Now tho' I cannot, with Mr. *Dennis,* think there is any ſuch ſtrict Relation between the Stage and the State, as that the Fall of the one muſt neceſſarily draw along with it the Ruin of the other: Or, with Mr. *Congreve,* apprehend any the leaſt Danger of running melancholy mad, falling foul on our ſelves, and cutting our own Wind-pipes, upon the ſhutting up of a Play-houſe: Yet I ever have been, and ſtill am of the Opinion, that Plays may very well be allow'd, and that in a Chriſtian Common-wealth too; as a Diverſion not only innocent, but inſtructive, ſuch a one indeed, as may rather contribute very much to the Promotion of Virtue, than any way countenance or incourage Vice.

But

But here I would not be misunder-stood.

By Plays, I do not mean all Plays; nor such neither, as those with which our Theaters have, of late Years, been but too plentifully furnish'd. No: Many of our Modern Poets have certainly been very much to blame; and have assum'd to themselves some very unjustifiable Liberties. They have err'd in Fundamentals, they seem to have made Choice of Characters only for their Lewdness, and have very frequently crown'd Vice with the Reward of Virtue. The Plays therefore that I mean, are such only as Mr. *Collier* himself means, when he tells us in the very Beginning of his Book, that *Their Business is to recommend Virtue, and discountenance Vice; To shew the Uncertainty of human Greatness, the sudden Turns of Fate, and the unhappy Conclusions of Violence and Injustice: 'Tis to expose the Singularities of Pride and Fancy, to make Folly and Falshood contemptible, and to bring every thing that is ill under Infamy and Neglect.* A very honourable Testimony this of the great Excellence and Usefulness of Dramatick Poetry! A remarkable Concession, believe me! especially so plac'd, in the very Front of a Book levell'd against the Stage.

Introd. to his View.

Stage. Here, indeed, Mr. *Collier* has allow'd our Poets Elbow-room enough:
Here is a Field, large enough in all Conscience, for the moſt unruly Fancy to
range in; and yet no body, I think, can
juſtly blame either our Poets or our Plays,
whilſt they keep themſelves ſtrictly within theſe Limits; Mr. *Collier* at leaſt, of
all Men living, ought not to do it. But
the Matter is quite otherwiſe, the Gentleman is ſomething Squeamiſh, and conſequently very hard to be pleas'd; he will
not be contented with a Stage, tho' of
his own modelling; and therefore what
he ſays here, he deſires, I ſuppoſe, ſhould
be look'd upon only as an ingenious
Flouriſh; one of thoſe many Rhetorical
Harrangues, with which his Book is
every where embelliſh'd even to exceſs:
And all, brought in like this, only by way
of Aggravation, to ſet the Poets, and their
Sins in a fairer Light, and then afterwards laſh them at his Pleaſure.

For if any of thoſe Gentlemen, ſhould
happen to lay hold on that his Conceſ-
ſion, with a deſign to make uſe of it as
a Rule, or Standard, by which they might,
with Safety, venture to regulate all their
future Performances for the Stage; why
then he is their Humble Servant, he
knows nothing at all of the Matter, but

pre-

prefently flies off; very couragiously bids
Defiance to all Plays in general; and at
laft appears in Triumph againft them, at
the Head of a vaft multitude of Authorities, drawn all from Philofophers, Orators, and Poets; from Councils, Fathers,
and *French* Bifhops; from Imperial Conftitutions, Acts of Parliament and *Dutch*
Gazetts; nothing in fhort can efcape his
Diligence, that feems to look but never
fo little a-fquint upon the Stage.

I do very willingly own, that upon my
firft reading Mr. *Collier*'s Book, I knew
not well what Judgment to make of it.
I thought indeed his Stile a little too
warm for a Reformer, and yet I could
not find, that he any where openly declar'd himfelf an Enemy; 'till looking a
little nearer into his Quotations from the
Fathers, I perceiv'd that feveral of them,
feem'd to bear full as hard againft the
Stage it felf, as againft the Abufes of it.
And then I firft began to fufpect, that
he aim'd at fomething more in his Book,
than he pretended to in his Title Page.
And I was very much confirm'd in that
Opinion, upon reading his *Reply to
Mr.* Congreve's *Amendments,* and the
Vindication of the Author of the Relapfe;
where he fully explains, what was not fo
very intelligible in his *View;* and makes
his

his Defign againft all Plays in general, vifible enough. However, fince it is plain that Mr. *Collier* has plaid faft and loofe, all along appearing fhy of declaring his real Sentiments concerning the Legality, or Illegality of Plays; infomuch, that 'tis no eafie matter to guefs what he would be at; I fhall in the profecution of this Difcourfe, confider him firft as a Reformer only of our Plays; and then as a profeft Enemy to all. And I doubt not but I fhall make it very plainly appear, that in the prefent Cafe, he's neither a fair Reformer, nor a formidable Enemy. I muft confefs, I look upon his Book as one of the fevereft Satyrs againft the Stage, and the Stage-Poets, as he's pleas'd to call them, that ever yet appear'd in Publick. But then 'tis only a Satyr; that is, a Piece made up of a great deal of Wit, fome Truth, and little or no Argument. But to proceed:

Mr. *Collier,* as a Reformer, is pleas'd in the firft Place to find Fault with our Plays, for the Ranknefs, and Indecency of their Language; and fo has given us a whole Chapter under the Title

Of the Immodesty of the Stage.

View, p. 3.   He begins thus; *In treating this Head,*
I hope the Reader does not expect I should
set down Chapter and Page; and give
him the Citations at length.   And pray
why not? Why he presently gives you
Ibid.   his Reason, and says, *To do this would*
be a very unacceptable and foreign Em-
ployment.   Neither the one, nor the o-
ther, in my poor Opinion.   No more
foreign, than for a Judge, at the Assizes,
to call for a Malefactor to the Bar; nor
less acceptable, I dare answer for it, than
many of his other Quotations from the
Poets.

For there are but very few Readers,
but what would bear every whit as well
with an Entertainment of Smut, or Bawdy, as of Blasphemy, or Atheism. He
Ibid.   goes on still with his Reasons. *Indeed*
the Passages, many of them, are in no
Condition to be handled: He that is desi-
rous to see these Flowers, let him do it in
their own Soil; 'tis my Business rather to
kill the Root than transplant it. Well
then: It is not now his Reader, that
Mr. *Collier* pretends to Compliment on
this Occasion, but himself; he's horribly
afraid,

afraid, it feems, of fouling his own Fingers. A very ftrange Averfion fure this Gentleman muft have againft all Smut. For he's abfolutely refolv'd to prevent the Spreading of it, whatever it may coft him; nay rather than fail, he will kill the pernicious Weed in the Root; whilft at the fame time he very liberally tranfplants thofe choicer Flowers of Prophanefs, Blafphemy, and Atheifm; for a further Increafe, one would think, of thofe rare and admirable Virtues. If this be not ftraining at a Gnat, and fwallowing a Camel, for my part I know not what is? Well:

But tho' Smut may be abominable, nafty and naufeous; and in Mr. *Collier's* Opinion, infectious too beyond all other things in the World, yet he prefently begins to fhake off fome of thofe difmal, melancholy Apprehenfions of its Malignancy ty, with which at firft he feem'd fo ftrangely poffefs'd; he brisks up a little, and will at laft venture his Reader, tho' not himfelf. *He will point to the Infection*   Ibid. *at a diftance, he will refer in general to* Play *and* Perfon, where the Curious, at their own Peril, may be fatisfy'd, whether he any ways wrongs the Poets or no. Now what is all this Stir and Noife; all this affected Precaution for? unlefs on purpofe to prepoffefs his Reader, with the

the Heinousness of those Crimes in our
Poets, which yet, at the same time, he
desires to be excus'd from proving against
them.   But he hopes, I suppose, by stop-
ping his own Nose, and crying out a
Stink, to fright others from running theirs,
too far, into those Ordures which he here
first pretends to start at, and afterwards
Harangues against, for several Pages together.   For if those Hopes do not deceive
him, then indeed he gains a very considerable Point; his Word will be taken
in the Case, which is just the thing he
aims at ; and then those merry Gentlemen, the Poets, must expect no Quarter.
They shall be represented as black, not as
they are only, but as all the Wit Mr. *Col-*
lier has can make them.   Whereas had
he been oblig'd to produce their own
Words, perhaps the Smut might not
have appear'd altogether of so deep a Dye,
and so some of his Readers, might possibly have been dull enough not to apprehend, and others so careless, as to over-
look the Venom; and then Mr. *Collier* had
been finely serv'd indeed, two Parts, at
least, of three of his following Harangues
had been utterly spoil'd. For believe me,
there must go something more than a
plain downright dry Quotation, to rig
out all this unlucky Smut exactly for his
Pur-

Purpofe; there muft be Glofs, and Comment, a great deal of turning and wind-
ing, ftretching and improving, before it
will appear half fo dreadful as he would
willingly reprefent it. Now tho' Mr. *Collier* be well enough acquainted with all
thofe little Arts, and can make ufe of
them too upon other Occafions; yet Mo-
defty, and common Decency, would not
permit a Perfon of his Character to do it
on this. And there you have the very
beft Reafon I can think of, and as good
a one perhaps, as Mr. *Collier* himfelf can
give you, for his extraordinary Nicety in
this Particular. Now tho' I cannot but
think Mr. *Collier* has dealt very hardly
with our Poets, in endeavouring to render them fo extreamly black as he has
done, and that upon a general Accufa-
tion only; fo that, even in that refpect,
he may be look'd upon as no very fair
Reformer; yet that is not what I mean,
I do not infift upon it. For had he been
never fo particular in his Quotations, I
fhould not have thought my felf any otherwife oblig'd to have taken notice of them;
than to have agreed with him in the Cenfure of whatever had appear'd to be evidently ill: Since I do not in the leaft pretend, to defend any thing our Poets may
have written that is really blameable;
and

and all Smut I take to be so, that is spoken never so little out of Character.

My Design, as I've already hinted, is to shew that Mr. *Collier*, even whilst he's Reforming our Plays, whilst he pretends to be aiming * only at the Abuses; makes ever now and than so home a Thrust at the Stage it self, as might prove Mortal, were his Arguments, but half so keen, as his Wit. Some of those by-Strokes we have under this Head, but not many; and those rather dark and remote Hints, than plain positive Assertions. For he yet keeps pretty well within the Bounds of Moderation. He has not yet roused up his Anger, nor lash'd himself into a Fury; but he warms apace, 'till at last enrag'd by Opposition, his Passion quite blinds his Reason, and confounds his Judgment. To give you therefore a true Taste of Mr. *Collier's* manner of Reforming Language of our Plays; I shall here take Notice of some of those more remarkable Passages in his *Reply* to Mr. *Congreve's* Amendments, as are by no Means to be neglected, and yet are no where so properly to be consider'd, as under this present Head of the *Immodesty of the Stage.* But before I do that, give me leave to shew you, as briefly as I can, the great Weakness of those

* B. *prima*
fol. 9.

few

few Objections he has made, in this Chapter, against all Smut in Plays. This perhaps may be thought something foreign to my present Purpose; but having Mr. *Collier's* Example, and Excuse too, for the Digression, I shall proceed; and that, without any manner of Apprehension that any of my Readers should so far mistake my Design; as to think that I thereby pretend to defend that Vice which he so very feebly attacks.

Pref. to his Reply to Mr. Cong. Amend.

In the first Place therefore, he tells us Smut is dangerous: *Such licentious Discourse tends to no Point, but to Stain the Imagination, or awaken Folly, and to weaken the Defences of Virtue.* This Argument may indeed hold good against all Smut wantonly, and lavishly brought in, or spoken out of Character; and consequently, against several of those extravagant, and unwarrantable Liberties, which many of our modern Poets, have pretended in that Particular.

View, p. 9.

But in a well regulated Play, where nothing of Smut is heard, but from the Mouth of some infamous Person; and that too, all along ridicul'd, censur'd, or discourag'd, and at the last severely punish'd: I cannot see any the least Probability of that Danger he speaks of. But to this Point, I shall have occasion

to

to speak more hereafter; this being the only Argument he brings, either against the Stage it self or its Abuses, that seems to have any thing of Weight in it. Well:

View, p. 6.8.

But the Danger of Smut is but part of the Objection, 'tis all Scandal and Meanness into the Bargain, 'tis a Fault in Behaviour as well as Religion. In other Instances, Vice is often but too fashionable; but here a Man cannot be a Sinner, without being a Clown. And is Mr. *Collier* sure of his Hand here? I doubt not. For tho' Smut, where either the Terms are foul and offensive, or the Sense such as conveys too gross an Idea to the Imagination; may be, as he says, but a Rustick, and uncreditable Talent: Yet if we look a little nearer into the Matter, I believe we may find that Smut, when the Expression is clean, and the Wit clear, has been often admitted into better Company than Mr. *Collier's* aware of. This tho' it may be difficult enough to prove, yet I shall here give you such an Instance of, and that from a Play too, as I do not at all question, will be allow'd to be Authentick enough. The Play is, *The Man of Mode,* or *Sir* Fopling Flutter; where Mrs. *Herriot,* a lively, brisk, young Heiress; but withal a Person of great Honour, and Virtue, being Cour-

Courted by *Dorimant,* a Gentleman of Senfe, Wit, and Breeding, tho' otherwife a Libertine: After fome Difcourfe goes on thus.

Herr. *To Men who have fared in this Town like you, 'twou'd be a great Mortification to live on Hope: Cou'd you keep a Lent for a Miftrefs?*

Dor. *In Expectation of a happy* Eafter; *and tho' Time be very precious, think forty Days well loft, to gain your Favour.*

Now, tho' the firft hint be here given by a Woman; and both Queftion, and Anfwer, are at the Bottom Smutty and Prophane, yet is there nothing in either, fo plain or grofs, as may feem to border, in the leaft, on Rufticity, or ill Manners: And tho' all the World muft allow *Dorimant* lewd, and a Sinner; yet no body, I am confident can be fo dull as to miftake him for a Clown. Sir *George Etheridge,* as a Gentleman, and a Courtier, was too well skill'd in all the Niceties of a genteel Converfation; and as a Poet, ever too true to his Characters, to to fail fo grofly in the Conduct of one of the chiefeft of 'em.

But tho' we will not allow Smut to be either dangerous, or clownifh, yet he's very confident we muft, with him, look on it as Unnatural in the Mouth of a

Woman;

Woman; all Women, if you'll believe
him, being by Nature so modest, that
it is a great Error, if not a Sin, to sup-
View, p. 9. pose them otherwise. *For to represent them*
without this Quality, is to make Monsters
of them and throw them out of Character.
Strongly possess'd, and wonderfully pleas'd
with the Novelty, I suppose, of the Conceit; he presently regalls the Ladies with
a very remarkable Harangue upon Modesty. He tells them, *It is the distin-*
guishing Virtue of their Sex; Very true;
and serves both for Ornament and Defence.
Who denies it? *It was design'd,* he says,
by Providence as a Guard to Virtue, and
that it might be always at hand, 'twas
wrought into the Mechanism *of the Body.*
Very likely indeed! and that no doubt
of it is the Reason, that there are so very few impudent Women in the World;
and that they are as rarely to be met
with in this our Island, as Wolves,
Bears or Tygers. But to be serious; I
must confess, I ever looked upon the
great Modesty of the generality of our
Women, to have been the happy Effect
rather of a pious, careful, and wary Education, than of any thing extraordinary
in the Contexture of their Bodies. And
thought it a Virtue imprinted on their
tender Minds first by their Parents; improv'd

prov'd afterwards by their own Reafon, and the prevailing Dictates of a holy Religion; and all along confirm'd, ftrengthen'd, and increas'd by the good Grace of an ever-merciful God. If I have hitherto been in an Error, as foon as ever I am convinced of it, I fhall readily embrace Mr. *Collier's* Doctrine, which is certainly very Courtly, but how Sound, there's the Queftion? In the mean Time, I hope he will excufe me if I cannot miftake a meer Poetical, frothy Harangue, for a fubftantial Argument.

I could eafily clear my Way to the End of this long Flourifh, but that I am afraid of trefpafling too much on the Patience of my Reader. I fhall therefore leave it to the Ladies to be commended, perhaps, by thofe that do underftand it; and admir'd by thofe that do not. 'Tis now time for me to remember my Promife, and to take fome Notice of a bold, and as our Author himfelf thinks, a concluding Stroke or two of his, not only againft all Immodefty, but even ordinary Freedom of Converfation and innocent Jefting too, on the Stage. Here indeed, he feems to be for fcrewing up the Players, to the feverer Difcipline of the *Carthufian* Monks, and reducing all their Converfation within the narrow Compafs

C

pass of a *Memento Mori*: Or, rather he pretends, at one Blow, to strike both the Stage, and Stage-Poets Dumb.

Mr. *Congreve*, in his *Amendments*, contending for some certain Liberties to be allow'd, and that from *Aristotle*'s own *Definition of Comedy*; Mr. *Collier* first pretends to bring that great Man over to his Party, and then proceeds thus; *But supposing* Aristotle *more liberal to Mr.* Congreve, *what Service would it do him? Does not Christianity refine the Pleasures, and abridge the Liberties of Heathenism?* Yes, certainly: But what of all that? Christianity does indeed Refine our Pleasures, but not as Mr. *Collier* Reforms Plays; it does not take them quite away. For certainly there are several Diversions, several innocent Liberties, that a good Christian may pretend to, and yet no Wrong done to his Profession neither. But Mr. *Collier* goes on, *St.* Paul *bids us put away all Filthiness, and foolish Talking, and that such Things ought not so much as to be nam'd amongst Christians.* How! ought they not so much as to be nam'd? and must these Words of the Apostle be taken in a strict literal Sense? What then will become of Mr. *Collier* himself? who in the very same Page, not only names, but very freely gives up

Reply to
Mr. Cong.
Amend.
P. 8.

Cove-

Covetousness to Satan, or which in his Opinion is much at one, to the Stage-Poets to make Sport with. However, upon the whole Matter, Mr. *Collier* presumes that he has got St. *Paul* on his Side, and so in a very good Humour, he presently puts two or three smart Questions to Mr. *Congreve;* with which, our Christian Reformer, very wisely supposes he may have put the Heathen Poet to a Nonplus. *When Revelation says one Thing, and Paganism another, how are we to determine? Is not an Apostle's Testimony more cogent than that of a Philosopher? and the new Testament, above all the Rules of* Aristotle *or* Horace? Yes, yes; or of Mr. *Collier* either. And therefore let us see what the * Apostle does say, as well as what Mr. *Collier* would have him say. The Apostles Words are these, *But Fornication, and all Uncleanness, or Covetousness, let it not be once nam'd amongst you, as becometh Saints.*

Neither Filthiness, nor foolish Talking, nor Jesting, which are not convenient; but rather giving of Thanks.

Now the Use that Mr. *Collier* would make of these Words, is to shew that Filthiness, or Obscenity of Speech, foolish Talking, nay, and all Jesting too, are, not only, not to be us'd; but not so much

Reply to Mr. Cong. Amend. P. 9.

* St. Paul. Ephes. 5. 3.

4.

as

as to be nam'd amongſt Chriſtians. This,
if it be St. *Paul's* Meaning, is more than
I yet ever heard of. I never before knew
that our Religion oblig'd us to be dull,
or that a Chriſtian could not break a Jeſt
without breaking a Commandment too.
But if it be ſo, why then a long Farewel
to all Plays indeed! Filthineſs, or Obſcenity of Speech, and idle Jeſting, ſhall
preſently ſweep all our Comedies; and
then, with a very little of Mr. *Collier's*
Management, fooliſh Talking will do juſt
as much for our Tragedies. For if honourable, virtuous Love, be, as he very
frequently and plainly tells us, but a whin-
ing, ſneaking, ſnivelling, dangerous, and
deſtructive Paſſion: Ambition, Glory,
Grandeur of Soul, and other ſuch like
Heroick Qualities, nothing elſe but Folly and Pride, trickt up in a Play-houſe
Diſguiſe: How can any thing our beſt
Poets can ſay on thoſe Topicks, but fall
under the Cenſure of fooliſh Talking?
And then take away Love, and Heroes,
and what has a Stage-Poet left to work
upon? Why, very little, or nothing, I
do aſſure you; but all Matters will then
go very glibly on, as Mr. *Collier* would
have them: Our Stage-Poets, Stage-Plays,
and Stage-Players too, will be all ſilenc'd,
and utterly confounded for ever.

View, p. 50, 287.
Reply to Mr. Cong. Amend. p. 34, 85.

But

But to do this wonderful Feat compleatly and effectually, Mr. *Collier,* I doubt muft ftrain hard, and ftretch our Apoftle's Meaning to a much higher Pitch, than he ever intended. For unlefs he can perfuade us, that St. *Paul* forbids all obfcene, filthy, foolifh, Talking and Jefting, under the fame Penalty that he does Fornication, actual Uucleannefs, or Covetoufnefs; I cannot fee how thofe Words, by him quoted, can do half the intended Execution; and yet, how he can poffibly make that out, for my part I cannot imagine. Since in the fifth Verfe of the Chapter before us, which is but a Recapitulation of thofe Crimes, which that great and glorious Apoftle, tells the *Ephefians,* would certainly exclude them from the Kingdom of Chrift, and of God; he very plainly and diftinctly repeats Fornication, Uncleannefs, and Covetoufnefs, but not a Word of obfcene, filthy, foolifh, or idle Talking and Jefting. But to give you the full, clear and true Meaning of St. *Paul* in this Place; I need do very little more than change the Order of his Words, and then you'll find that great Apoftle thus advifing and exhorting the *Ephefians: Brethren, be ye Followers of God as dear Children, and walking in Love, as Chrift alfo hath loved us.*

But

But as for Fornication, Uncleanneſs, or Covetouſneſs, let them not be once na-med amongſt you; not nam'd with Al-lowance, not nam'd with any Extenuati-on, not nam'd, but with ſome Deteſtati-on, as becometh Saints. For you well know that no Whoremonger, or unclean Perſon, nor covetous Man, who is an I-dolater, hath any Inheritance in the King-dom of God, or of Chriſt. Neither do you, my Brethren, give your ſelves over to, or incourage others in, obſcene, filthy, wanton Diſcourſes, fooliſh Talking, or unſeaſonable Jeſting; which are not con-venient. But rather ſpend your precious Time in Prayer to God, for all thoſe good Things you daily ſtand in need of, and in praiſing his holy Name, for all thoſe Blef-ſings he has already beſtow'd upon you.

Now if theſe Words, thus rang'd in this Order, and thus explain'd, do con-tain the true Meaning of our Apoſtle in this Place; then any one, I think, may eaſily enough diſcern the vaſt Difference St. *Paul* himſelf makes, between actual Uncleanneſs, and Obſcenity of Speech: That, being by him forbidden under the higheſt Penalty imaginable: This, as in-convenient, and then only criminal, or ſinful, when either us'd in Exceſs, by way of Incouragement to others, or, by

our

our selves, set up in Competition with our Duty to God.

It is a certain and undoubted Truth, that we are not to waste our Time, either in using or hearkening to wanton, lascivious Discourses, foolish Talking, or Jesting; no, nor in any other Diversion, or meer Recreation whatever. For how sweet, how charming, or how innocent soever that Diversion, or Recreation, may be in its own Nature, yet Loss of Time, or Neglect of any necessary Duty, will render it Criminal. Since the Care of our Souls, does most certainly require the greatest Part of our Time, tho' not absolutely all.

There are, I know, some few of the Fathers, that seem to run Things to a much greater height; that will allow of no Diversion, tho' never so innocent; nor admit of any Jest, tho' never so harmless; but look upon any, the least Mirth or Gaiety, as misbecoming the Gravity of a Christian Professor. But how far so much Severity may be allow'd of, to the Condemnation, I will not say of Plays only, but of all the very best, and most refin'd Conversation in the World; and what Scruples it may justly raise, in the Minds of several good, and

C 4   pious

pious Perſons, I leave to Mr. *Collier* himſelf to judge.

A certain reverend Commentator on the Epiſtles of St. *Paul,* taking particular Notice of their great Severity who condemn all innocent Jeſting, and will allow us Chriſtians, no other Diverſion than that of Sighs, and Tears; and wiſely foreſeeing the ill Conſequences of it, comes ſeaſonably in to our Relief, with a very learned Diſtinction. *Verum ne hæc Scrupuloſum quem faciant, intellige jocularitatem illam dedicere Chriſtianos, quæ nihil ſpectat quam ut riſum excitet. Si enim ulteriùs, aliâ, referatur, verbi gratia, ad honeſtam recreationem, lætitiam, animi excitationem, Sanitatem Corporis tuendam, ut ſcilicet homo alacrior fiat, vegetior, & aptior ad ſuas functiones, Deique obſequium, honeſta eſt, decetque Chriſtianos.* Now tho', for my own part, I cannot imagine where the great Hurt lies of laughing a little, now and then, tho' but for laughing ſake, yet I ſhall not quarrel with our Commentator on that account; but allow of his Diſtinction, and accept of the Liberty, he offers us, on his own Terms; which indeed are large enough to comprehend all innocent Diverſions whatſoever, and conſequently Plays,

C. C. A Lapide in Divi Pauli Epiſt. Com. *p. 526.*

Plays, as they may and ought to be Reform'd, that is, not by lopping or cutting off all vicious Characters from the
Stage, the thing Mr. *Collier* all along aims
at, but by an inviolable Obfervation of
a ftrict Stage-Difcipline ; by which nothing elfe is meant, but a conftant, proportionable Reward of Virtue, and Punifhment of Vice: For Plays, at leaft if
we may believe Mr. *Collier* himfelf, were
ever defign'd as an Amufement only, a
meer Diverfion; their great and chief
End ever was, and ftill is, Inftruction,
as he has taken fome Pains to prove; View, *p.*
and if fo, then, I think, we may fafely 161.
place 'em, for any thing he has faid to
the contrary, in the very Front of all innocent Diverfions whatfoever. Innocent,
I fay, and that too, tho' the Poet fhould
now and then bring in a Whore, a Bawd,
or a Pimp upon the Stage, and make
their Converfation, in fome meafure, an-
fwerable to their Characters.

But now, there being little lefs under
this Head to be confider'd, unlefs the Attempt he has made to prove the Ancient
Heathen Poets, more referv'd, as to the
Point of Smut, and more modeft than a-
ny of our modern, Chriftian Writers; for
which he has been already call'd to Account by another Hand, I fhall take my
leave

leave of this, and proceed to his next
Chapter, where he complains of

The Prophaness of the Stage.

And this Charge, he says, may come
under these Two Particulars.

First, Their Cursing and Swearing.

Secondly, Their Abuse of Religion, and
holy Scripture.

Under the first of these Particulars, he
observes the very same Method, as under the former Head of the *Immodesty of
the Stage.* He produces none of those
Oaths he so much complains of, but first
draws up a general Charge; then harangues a while upon that Charge, and
at last, without any more Ceremony, very roundly proceeds to Condemnation.
Indeed, he seems to be grievously offended at their frequent Cursing, and
Swearing in their Plays. And as he very rhetorically sets forth the Matter, one
would be apt to think the whole three
Hours Diversion of the Stage, were no-
View,*p.56.*thing else but a confus'd hellish Consort
of prophane Ranting and Roaring, Swear-
ing and Cursing, Tearing and Damning.
And yet after all this mighty Noise, he
produces but half a dozen of our loosest
Come-

Comedies as guilty; three of which, he represents as faulty only, and the other three as rampantly scandalous in that Particular. From whence any unprejudic'd Reader may observe, that of above a thousand Plays in Print, there are but six, that he himself thinks can justifie his Complaint, and of all our Modern Writers, but three that can come up to that charitable Character, he has been pleas'd to give the World of them. For I know not by what Fault, or Misfortune of theirs it so happens, but certainly he either is, or would be thought to be, a most inveterate Enemy to all Poets. He very industriously ransacks their Plays, catching at every little Slip of the Pen, that can look like anything either lewd or prophane; and not contented with that, he follows them to their Prologues and Dedications; he pursues them to their Translations, and Miscellany Poems; and when he has nothing else left to cavil at, as if there were something of Immorality in that too, he lashes them, at last, for their Dulness.

But to return to the Business in hand, he for his part thinks those six Plays enough to settle the Matter of Fact; and as for the Point of Law, he goes on thus, *I hope there needs not many Words to* View, p. 57. *prove Swearing a Sin.* What! all Swearing?

ing? I hope our Author is not turn'd
Quaker? But let that pass, we will not
fall out about small Matters, I'll rather
take his Meaning, without holding him
too strictly to his Words; and indeed
he does in some measure explain himself,
whilst he continues thus. *What is more*
provoking than Contempt? And what Sin
more contemptuous than common Swearing?
But can there then be no Oaths us'd on
the Stage, but what must necessarily im-
ply a Contempt of God? When a Poet
represents Swearing, in the Person of
some Wicked, Atheistical Wretch, as
odious, scandalous, and sinful; and at
last too, punishes the Wretch for Swearing; and all with a design of deterring
others from falling into so detestable a Sin;
can an Oath, or two, in such a Case,
be look'd on as contemptuous, by any
Man that is in his right Senses? But
Mr. *Collier,* I suppose, either has not stu-
died the Case, or else is unwilling to deliver his Opinion upon it. For he still
follows his first Blow, and says, *What*
can be more Insolent and Irreligious, than
to bring in God to attest our Trifles, to
give Security for our Follies, and to make
a Part of our Diversion? They that bring
Oaths upon the Stage with any such abominable Design, deserve to be punish'd
here,

Ibid.

View, p, 58.

here, and will certainly fmart for it hereafter.   But in the mean time, Mr. *Collier*
feems to forget, that in the very next
Chapter to this but one, he gives his
Reader the Diverfion of eight or ten whole
Pages, at leaft, only to prove Inftruction
to be the chief End of Plays; which, as I
take it, alters the Cafe very much.   But
he goes on, *To play with Majefty and*   Ibid.
Omnipotence is to render it cheap and
contemptible.   Very true, and therefore
the Cafe I have propos'd, fuppofes no
fuch Matter; but may very well confift
with the Belief of Providence, and Revelation.   But all this is nothing, there
is fomething coming, that is certainly very extraordinary; for he lifts up his Hand
high, and ftands in a menacing Pofture,
as if he doubted not, but to fell all our
Stage-Poets at a Blow; and now it falls.
The Poets are of all People moft to blame,
they want even the Plea of Bullies, and
Sharpers.   There's no Rancounters, no
Starts of Paffion, no fudden Accidents to
difcompofe them.   They Swear in Solitude,
and cool Blood, under Thought and Deli-
beration, for Bufinefs, and for Exercife.
This is a terrible Circumftance, it makes
all Malice Prepenfe, and inflames the
Guilt, and the Reckoning.   Here now I
cannot but wonder why Mr. *Collier* does

not as well tax our Poets with the Sin of
Lying, as that of Swearing. For certainly they every Day vent a great many
Untruths, and there are some People, I
doubt, not weak enough to be impos'd
upon by them; wherein, say our Casuists,
lyes all the Venom, all the Sin of a Lie.
But not a Word of that; for beside, the
Risk he was likely to run, of being
laugh'd at for his Pains; he very well
knew, that one and the same Reason
would excuse the Poets in either Case;
and that is this, that in neither, do they
speak their own Sense, or mean any Ill;
nor does their Heart go along with their
Pen. Tho' Mr. *Collier* would insinuate
the contrary, not only by this his charitable Harangue here, but when in another Place he says, *I wish they would consider, that it is the Poets that speak in
the Persons of the Stage.* And that indeed is very true: But are they therefore
suppos'd to speak their own Sentiments?
If so, What shall we say of Sir *John Den-
ham,* Sir *William D'Avenant,* and my
Lord *Orery,* who when they laid their
Scenes amongst the *Turks,* or *Persians,*
were oblig'd to make their Persons speak
many things unfit for a Christian to utter, as directly contrary to his Faith?
Were they therefore to be look'd upon

Reply to
the Relap
p. 108.

as

as *Mahometans?* But to proceed, and speak more at large to this Particular Objection of Swearing, on the Stage.

There are but two things, that I know of, that make an Oath sinful. The first is, that Contempt which usually attends the Breach of any of God's Commands. The other is, the taking his Holy Name in vain; that is, when we rashly, tho' not contemptuously, make use of it in low, and trivial Matters. But in the Case by me propos'd, there is not any thing that can look like Contempt, much less can it be said that God's Name is there taken in vain; since the Swearing there suppos'd, is all design'd either as a fair Warning for others, not to follow an Example which is represented as Evil; or by the Infliction of some exemplary Punishment on the Person offending, as a Terror, to fright and scare them from it. And no body, I think, will deny but that in either Case, we may safely venture to use the Name of God, and that without any the least Danger of Prophaning it. Hitherto then, as you see, the Poet's Heart may be perfectly free from all Thoughts of Evil; and if so, surely the Pen only, without the Heart, cannot Sin. For Mr. *Collier* very well knows who 'twas that long since told us, that *Out of the Heart*

Matthew,
Chap. 15.
V. 19. *Heart of Men proceed evil Thoughts, Adulteries, Fornications, Murders,* &c. Thus, tho' the Hand indeed may kill, yet 'tis the Heart alone that can make that killing Murder: And tho' the Eye may like and look upon a beautiful Woman, yet the Heart muſt Luſt after her, before that Look becomes Adulterous.

And now, how can the Poet be ſaid to ſtand in need of the poor Plea of Bullies, and Sharpers, for putting an Oath, or two, or more it may be, into the Mouth of ſome profligate Wretch, or profeſt Atheiſt? How can his writing in cool Blood, under Thought, and Deliberation, inflame his Reckoning and his Guilt? When thereby only, he has the better Opportunity of conſidering ſeriouſly, and calmly reflecting on the Heinouſneſs of the Sin, of repreſenting it the more Ugly, and the more Odious, and of inventing ſuch a Puniſhment for it, as may hold ſome Proportion with the Enormity of the Crime. And ſo much for Swearing, as it may, or may not, be ſinful on the Stage.

His next Endeavour is to prove it unlawful. If, ſays he, *Religion ſignifies nothing, as I'm afraid it does with ſome People,* There's a gentle rap on the Pate for the Stage-Poet, *en paſſant, there is*
View, p.
58.
Law

Law as well as Gospel against Swearing.
For the preventing and avoiding of the 3 *Jac.* 1.
great Abuse of the Holy Name of God, Cap. 21.
in Stage-Plays and Enterludes. Be it en-
acted by our Sovereign Lord, &c. "That
" if at any time, or times, after this pre-
" sent Sessions of Parliament, any Person
" or Persons, do or shall in any Stage-
" Play, Enterlude, Shew, &c. jestingly
" or prophanely speak, or use the Holy
" Name of God, of Jesus Christ, or of
" the Holy Ghost, or of the Trinity,
" which are not to be spoken but with
" Fear and Reverence, shall forfeit for
" every such Offence, by him, or them
" committed, ten Pound, &c. And now
pray what does this Act say against any
thing that I have pretended to defend?
I am very sure it does not absolutely forbid all Swearing on the Stage; unless
Mr. *Collier* will affirm, that we cannot
Swear, but that at the same time we must
name the Name of God, of Jesus Christ,
the Holy Ghost, or of the Trinity. But that
I believe he will not pretend to do, because
he very well knows, that some of our
Poets swear frequently by Heav'n, and
sometimes too by Hell; nor can I see
how either of those Oaths, or any other
of the like Nature, are forbidden by this
Act. And therefore Mr. *Collier,* I think,

is very much miſtaken, when he tells us,

View, p. 59.
that *by this Act, not only direct Swearing, but all vain Invocation of the Name of God is forbidden.* For there is not the leaſt mention made in this Act, either of direct or indirect Swearing; and how then is it forbidden? Nay the very Invocation or Uſe of the Name of God on the Stage, is no otherwiſe prohibited, than as it may be jeſtingly, or prophanely abus'd there. And ſo I proceed to his next Objection.

Ibid.
Swearing, in the Play-Houſe, he ſays, *is an ungentlemanly, as well as an unchriſtianly Practice.* And why ſo? Why he tells you, *The Ladies make a conſiderable Part of the Audience, and that Swearing before Women, is reckon'd a Breach of good Manners, and therefore a Civil Atheiſt will forbear it.* Well then, in Mr *Collier's* Opinion the Ladies, and the Players, muſt make up but one civil Company; in which all the Decorums of a genteel, refin'd, and courtly Converſation, are to be religiouſly obſerv'd on all hands, and that under the higheſt Penalty; which Penalty, to compleat the Compliment, muſt be nothing leſs than the Frowns, and utter Diſpleaſure of thoſe Ladies, they may offend by their Rudeneſs and Ill-breeding. Very good; but

he

he goes on much at the same rate. *Be-* View, *p.* 60.
sides, Oaths are a boistrous and tempestu-
ous sort of Conversation, generally the
Effects of Passion, and spoken with Noise
and Heat. Well, these Players are certainly the rudest, roughest Fellows in the
World! And I wonder in my Heart, how
the Ladies dare ever venture into their
Company. But he carries the Jest yet farther, *Swearing looks like the Beginning of* Ibid.
a Quarrel, to which Women have an A-
version; as being neither arm'd by Nature,
nor disciplin'd by Custom, for such rough
Disputes. Very true indeed, our Ladies
are seldom train'd, either to the Sword,
Pike, or Musket; nor will the Weakness
of their tender Limbs, bear with the boi-
sterous Roughness of a *Cornish* Hug; and
therefore, to prevent some of their Fears,
and keep those roguy Players at Arms
length, there's a convenient Distance, a
large Pit, between the Stage and the
Boxes. But now comes the Top, the
very Cream of the Conceit. *A Woman* Ibid.
will start at a Soldier's Oath almost as
much as at the Report of his Pistol. Yes,
and some Men too, or Sir *George Ethe-* She wou'd
rege was as much mistaken in his Remark, if she cou'd, p. 4.
near thirty Years since, as our Author
may be now in his; and yet the Jest past
well enough then, but how it has been

receiv'd

receiv'd fince, at the fecond hand, I cannot tell. But to let that pafs ; Can
Mr. *Collier,* in good fober earneft, think
that our Ladies, wh n they go to the
Play-Houfe, defign nothing elfe but a
civil Vifit to the Players; and that the
Players are confequently oblig'd to keep
themfelves within the ftraiteft Limits,
even of the niceft Ceremony, obfervable
in other Places, before Perfons of their
Virtue, Rank, and Quality; and that
too, all the while they are pleas'd to honour them with their Company ? Will
our Ladies allow of nothing on the Stage,
but what they would admit of in their
own Apartments at home, or upon a
meer Ceremonious Vifit abroad ? Why
then they muft e'en be contented to wave
the Diverfion of the Theatre, there being
but very few Charaѐters to be met with,
but what may, in fome fort or other, offend againft fo much Nicety : And this
Argument of our Author's will hold e-
qually good againft every thing not allowable in a Civil, Ceremonious Converfation, as againft Swearing. Thus,
according to this Doѐtrine, even the moft
common Proftitute, muft renounce her
gay, airy, wanton Follies, and in the
Scene appear all Virtuous, Grave and
Modeft. The ranting, tearing, bluftring
　　　　　　　　　　　　　　Bully,

Bully, muſt there forget his Noiſe, and
be all Gentle, Soft, and Tame. The
Drunkard muſt by no means Roar, Reel,
or Hickup on the Stage. Nor the plain,
downright, clumſie Clown, dare to appear before the Ladies, 'till he has firſt
learnt to make his Honours. No Drums
or Trumpets muſt be heard; no private
Quarrels, or publick Wars, no Siege, no
Battel repreſented; and all this only for
fear of breaking in upon good Manners,
and offending the Ladies; who, according to this new Doctrine of Mr. *Collier's,*
muſt be thought not able to bear with
the meer Repreſentation only, of ſo many great and manifeſt Indecencies.

But this is all ſuch poor, ſuch wretch-
ed Stuff, that Mr. *Collier,* I doubt not,
would have been heartily aſham'd of it,
as too much below a Perſon of his Qua-
lifications; but that he could not well re-
ſiſt the Temptation of any thing, how
mean ſoever, that offer'd it ſelf, as any
way proper to ſerve his preſent Turn a-
gainſt the Stage. Indeed, Men of his
Parts ſeldom trifle for nothing, they generally, ſome way or other, find their
Account in it; as Mr. *Collier* may poſſibly have done here, where tho' his Argument be extreamly weak, yet whatever
it wants in Strength, is abundantly ſup-

D 3

ply'd

ply'd by the Malice of it. For by that
way of Arguing, Mr. *Collier* not only puts
a great Compliment on Female Quality
wholly at the Poets Expence, but does
all he can to make the Ladies out of
Conceit with the Stage, and give them
a turn, againſt ſome of the moſt innocent,
as well as the moſt uſual Diverſions of
the Theater. Nay, he aims at the total
Overthrow of Plays, cutting off ſo many neceſſary Characters from 'em, as
muſt leave the Stage quite naked, and
effectually ſilence the Stage-Poets. Since
under ſuch a Limitation as he propoſes,
they muſt either not write at all; or,
which is much at one in relation to the
Play-houſe, what they do write, muſt be
ridiculous and impertinent: As any Child,
I think, may plainly perceive, by what
has been already ſaid, without any farther Illuſtration, or Aggravation of the
Matter. And yet this is Mr. *Collier*'s Method of Reforming, which puts me, I
muſt confeſs, ſtrangely in mind of thoſe
Gentlemen Reformers, who about the
Middle of the laſt Century, ſo throughly Reform'd the Religion and Government of this our Land, that at laſt they
left little or nothing, either of the one,
or the other, in the Nation. In a Word,
had I nothing more to object againſt
    Mr. *Col-*

Mr. *Collier,* of this Nature, than this one Argument of his, in its full Extent; I doubt not but it would be enough to justifie my Charge, and make him appear, to all the World, no very fair Reformer.

I come now to his second Branch of the Prophaness of the Stage; which is, their Abuse of Religion, and Holy Scripture. And here, indeed, he's free enough of his Quotations, of which, tho' some perhaps might have escap'd the Censure of a less industrious, or a less severe Inquisitor than our Author; yet many of them are indeed extreamly scandalous, impious, and wicked. In the Censure of all which I heartily join with him, as spoken all out of Character, and as it were in Defiance of that Stage-Discipline, which alone can justifie the publick Representation of any thing lewd, smutty, or prophane. For where-ever any thing of that nature is any otherwise represented, than as scandalous and sinful, and consequently not punish'd as such in the Person offending; there that Representation must be altogether criminal, and inexcusable. Nay, that is not all neither, for 'tis not enough that Vice is punish'd; but the Punishment must be, in some measure, proportionable to the Offence. And when 'tis so, then I do

affirm,

affirm, that the Poet cannot be said to commit the Sin he reprefents; tho' Mr. *Collier* would infinuate the contrary, as pretending to have but a very mean Opinion of our Stage-Difcipline. My Defign being to juftifie the Ufe of all well regulated Plays in general, without engaging my felf in the Defence of any of thofe particular Abufes, of which fome of our Poets have been too juftly accus'd, will not permit me to take any farther Notice of Mr. *Collier's* numerous Quotations, produc'd under this Head, on that Occafion: I fhall therefore here take the Opportunity of difcovering my own Sentiments, touching a real Reformation of the Stage; fuch a Reformation, I mean, as fhall be no way deftructive of the Thing to be reform'd; nor meerly Notional and Theorectick, but eafie to be reduc'd into Practice. Now the due Obfervation of a ftrict and fevere Stage-Difcipline, being the only fure and certain Means, by which we can ever hope to attain to fuch a Reformation: In order to what I have propos'd, and to convince the World of our Author's many, and moft notorious Prevarications in that Matter, I fhall endeavour to prove the following Particulars.

Firft,

First, That even Mr. *Collier* himself has, at the Bottom, a more favourable Opinion of our Stage-Discipline, than he's willing to own.

Secondly, That under the Protection of this Stage-Discipline, the Poet may safely, and innocently, make use of vicious Characters. And,

Thirdly, That vicious Characters not only may, but many times ought, to be brought upon the Stage.

That Mr. *Collier* pretends to have but a very mean Opinion of the Discipline of the Stage, is plain enough from what he says in the Close of this Chapter. *Prophaness, tho' never so well corrected, is not to be endur'd; it ought to be banish'd without Proviso, or Limitation. No Pretence of Character or Punishment can excuse it, or any Stage-Discipline make it tolerable.* View, p. 96. Very well said indeed, and I could wish it had been as well prov'd too. But no matter for that; what he says here, is nothing to what is to come; this is only a preparatory Dash of his Pen, in order to make way for a bolder Stroke. For hitching on, by degrees, and encroaching, more and more, upon the Stage; he tells us in another Place, that *As for Smut and Prophaness, 'tis every way criminal, and infectious; and* Reply to Mr. Cong. Amend. p. 10.

*no Difcipline can attone for the Repre-
fentation.* So, now we have Smut join'd
with Prophanefs, and both alike privileg'd? But pray what Vice fhall our Stage-
Difcipline be thought fufficient to attone
for, if not for a little Smut? Why, none
at all; that I take to be his Meaning:
Very good! We fhall fee, by and by,
whether he be really of that Opinion or
not: Or if he be fo, at prefent, whether
he will continue long in that Mind.

By what has been already faid, touching the Difcipline of the Stage, 'tis plain
that the Poet, in a regular Play, muft not
only punifh all Vice, but punifh it fo too,
as that the Punifhment may hold fome
Proportion to the Offence. Now the
greateft Punifhments which, by the Laws
of Comedy, may be impos'd on Offenders, being but eafie, light and trivial,
in Comparifon with thofe the Tragedian
may inflict; 'tis evident from thence, that
the Comick Writer is moft confin'd, and
therefore ought to be more wary, both
in the Choice of his Characters, and in
the Point of Converfation, than the
other. And yet our Comick Poets
have been, in a manner, the only Offenders. For they often wrong their beft
and nobleft Characters, whilft they very frequently make their Women of Quality,

lity, and Virtue, talk downright Bawdy;
and their fine accomplish'd Gentlemen,
their Heroes, prophane in their Court-
ship, lewd and irreligious in their Conversation, in a word, most notorious Li-
bertines. And after all, so far are they
from punishing of them, that for the
most part, those very worthy Gentlemen
are represented as successful in all their
Attempts. No wonder then, that some
of our modern Comedies have afforded
Mr. *Collier* such a plentiful Crop of Weeds,
as he has expos'd to the World. And
indeed, 'tis observable that most, if not
all Mr. *Collier*'s Quotations, are either taken from Comedies, or else from such
Tragedies, as are irregular in the Distri-
bution of Rewards and Punishments. Nay
he seems industriously to avoid all those
Plays, how lewd, or how prophane soever they may be, where that one necessary Rule, of rewarding the Good and
punishing the Bad, is any thing tolerably
observ'd. Otherwise, how came the *Li-*
bertine to escape his Censure? A Play,
whose very Title promis'd him work e-
nough; and where he might have met
with as great Variety, of Smut, Prophaness, Blasphemy, and Atheism, as in
any three of those Plays he has taken
so much Pains to expose. But the Cata-
strophe

ftrophe was there too exemplary, too terrible, and too amazing for his Purpose; he cared not to meddle with it. There, after Don *John* had for a long time triumph'd in his Lewdnefs, the Earth at laft opens; and fending forth vaft Flafhes of terrifying Flames, receives the trembling Atheift into her gaping, flaming Bowels. For there indeed the Poet did well, and wifely ftretch the Laws of Comedy, rather than fuffer fo much Wickednefs to go off with a lefs remarkable Punifhment.

To inftance but in one Play more, of a great many that offer themfelves. How came he to pafs by the *Villain,* an admirable Tragedy? unlefs becaufe *Maligny,* after all his Wickednefs, appears at laft impal'd alive upon a Stake, as a juft Reward due to his moft notorious Crimes.

Now, I muft confefs, when I confider his many Omiffions of this kind, which to me feem wilful; and that how flight foever he pretends to make of our Stage-Difcipline, yet he cares not to attack any of thofe Plays, where it appears in its full Vigour; I cannot but think he has, at the Bottom, a better Opinion of it, than he cares to own. For had he been really convinc'd in his Judgment, that

that no Punishment, no Stage Discipline, could attone for the Representation of any thing smutty or prophane; then certainly he ought to have produc'd some of his Instances, at least, from those Plays, where that Discipline had been religiously observ'd, and have rallied all his Forces against them. That had been great, that had been an Attempt worthy of Mr. *Collier.* He had then indeed struck at the Root of the Play-house, shaken the very Foundation of the Stage, and, if successful in his Blow, had gain'd an absolute Victory over all our Poets. But alas! he never intended to give himself that trouble, he had too fair, too easie a Game to play against those few of our modern Writers, who had unwarily enough neglected that Discipline; and too deep a Design against the Stage, to hazard all his Hopes upon such an Uncertainty.

Whoever reads, and seriously considers Mr. *Collier*'s *View,* will, I believe, be apt enough to conclude, that it was never any part of his Meaning, to Reform our Poets, but rather to render 'em as odious as possibly he could. For so eagerly he seems, all along, to pursue that Design, that he cares not by what Methods he does it, so it be done effectually:

&ctually : Even that very Stage-Difcipline,
which by no means he will allow fufficient to attone for the flighteft of their
Faults, fhall do Wonders, whenever he
can meet with an Opportunity of urging
it, as an Aggravation of them. Then 'tis
all in all with him, it not only alleviates,
and extenuates the greateft Guilt, but
attones for the moft horrid Impieties
that can be reprefented on a Stage, and
renders them perfectly innocent and
harmlefs. Thus when he mufters up his
Heathen Poets, as a Reproach and
Shame to our Chriftian Writers, tho'
he finds them all, more or lefs guilty of
the fame Faults, for which he fo feverely reflects on ours ; yet he very fairly ac-
quits them of the Guilt, upon the account
of their Stage-Difcipline.

I fhall produce but one or two Inftan-
ces, and then leave the Reader, as he
likes 'em, to confult Mr. *Collier's View*
for more of the fame Strain; where from
p. 86, to *p.* 94, he cannot look amifs.
Our Author paffes over the *Latin* Poets
flightly enough, as not fo very fit for his
View, p. 87. Purpofe; but then he tells us, *The* Greek
*Trajedians are more ftaunch, and write
nearer the Scheme of a natural Religion :
'Tis true they have fome bold Expreffions,
but then they generally reprove the Liberty,*

ty, and *punish the Men.* Very good:
Pray obſerve that, there's our Stage-Diſcipline to a Tittle: And, to mend the
Matter, you will ſee preſently, that ſome
of thoſe bold Expreſſions he ſpeaks of,
were notoriouſly prophane, blaſphemous,
and atheiſtical. For *Prometheus,* in *Æ-
ſchylus,* hectors, bluſters, and ſcorns to
ſubmit to *Jupiter* himſelf; and *Ajax,* in
Sophocles, when his Father advis'd him
to be brave, but religious withal, impi-
ouſly, and inſolently reply'd, that it was
for Cowards only to beg the Aſſiſtance
of the Gods; as for his part, he hop'd to
Conquer without them. And accordingly, when *Minerva* actually offer'd her
Help, he bid her mind her own Buſineſs,
he wanted no Goddeſs to aſſiſt him. And
yet after all theſe impious Sallies, Mr. *Collier* very fairly, and roundly delivers his
Opinion of theſe Plays in thoſe Words.
Upon the whole Matter, the Plays of View. p. 93.
Æſchylus, *and* Sophocles, *were form'd
upon Models of Virtue. They join Innocence, and Pleaſure, and deſign the Im-
provement of the Audience.* What! were
thoſe atheiſtical Rants then of *Prometheus* in the one, and *Ajax* in the other,
nothing? Or, as Mr. *Collier* ſeems to in-
ſinuate, did thoſe Poets think ſuch Im- View. p. 86.
piety allowable, *Becauſe the Characters*

of

of their Gods were not without Blemish?
Or did they ignorantly fall into those
Faults, *Because their Prospect of the
other World was but dim, nor were they
under the Terrors of Revelation?* By no
Means: For we find, that notwithstanding the recorded Infirmities of their
Gods, whatever their Notions of another
World might be, and tho' they were not
under those Terrors of Revelation that
we are; yet they had as great a Horror,
for all such bold Impieties, as we can have.
Else why did the one punish *Prometheus,*
and the other *Ajax?* Why, I say, if
they thought those Atheistical Expressions of theirs no Faults, did they punish
them at all? Or if they thought them but
slight ones, why did they punish them so
very severely? for their Punishment was
not only extreamly rigorous, but represented as judicial, and immediately proceeding from the just Anger of their offended Gods. And here I desire to know,
what any Christian could have done more,
in such a Case, to have express'd his real
Sense, and hearty Detestation of such
horrid Crimes? From what has been said
then, I think it appears plainly enough,
that both *Æschylus,* and *Sophocles,*
ador'd those very Deities they insulted
in their Plays, with the same Zeal, the
                                        same

fame Devotion, that we do the only true
and living God; that they thought themfelves, by their Religion, oblig'd to as
great an Abhorrency of all Prophaneneſs,
Blaſphemy, or Atheiſm, as we can be by
ours; and conſequently were then as
guilty, as any of our Modern Poets
would be now, that ſhould pretend to the
fame Liberty. What tho' their Religion
and their Gods too were all falſe? Could
that excuſe them that believ'd them all
true; and from their Hearts really and
religiouſly ador'd, reverenc'd, and re-
ver'd them as ſuch? I am confident
Mr. *Collier* will not ſay it. We muſt then
look for ſome other Excuſe for their Practice, and his Approbation of it; and
what better Excuſe can be alledg'd, than
that very Stage-Diſcipline, which he
himſelf tells us they moſt religiouſly obſerv'd. *Æschylus,* ſays he, *to make all* Vicw,p.88.
ſure, brings Prometheus *to Execution before the End of the Play. He diſcharges
Thunder and Lightning at his Head, ſhakes
his Rock with an Earthquake, turns the
Air into Whirlwinds, and draws up all
the Terrors of Nature to make him an Example. And* Ajax's *Deſtruction is repreſented as judicial; in* Sophocles, 'twas in-
flicted for his Pride, and Atheiſm; his
Inſolence made* Minerva *hate h m, and*
E   *was*

was the Cause of his Madness, **and** *Self-Murder:* This Stage-Discipline then it was that those Poets wholly depended on for their Indemnity, and which Mr. *Collier* has pronounc'd sufficient to atone for all those horrid Impieties. And indeed, since those Poets brought those great Examples of Irreligion on the Stage, with a good and pious Design, with an Intent, by their Punishment, to terrisie others from the like Wickedness; where was that Malice, where was that Contempt of their Gods, which alone could render them Criminal? And why then shall not the same Discipline atone for the same Offence in a Christian Writer? Since in such a Representation, under such Circumstances, there can be no Crime, no Sin committed, either against God or his own Conscience. And so much for my first Particular. I come now to prove my second, *viz.* That vicious Characters, such as Pimps, Whores, Bawds, and Cheats in Comedies; great and illustrious Villains, wicked and irreligious Princes, Atheists and Apostates in Tragedies, may safely and innocently be brought on the Stage. Now to prove this, one would think, I need use no other Argument, than the constant Practice of all Poets, and the Approbation of all Ages.

I

I do not say, of all People in all Ages; no, I know too well, that almoſt in every Age there have appear'd ſome Enemies, ſome ſuch Reformers as Mr. *Collier.* And yet, notwithſtanding all their ſubtile undermining Arts, all their moſt eager Attempts againſt the Stage, Plays have not only been allow'd, but countenanc'd and incourag'd, and have flouriſh'd under the Protection of moſt of the greateſt Princes and beſt Patriots in the World; and that too, without any Exceptions taken at that Liberty the Poets ever pretended to in the Choice of their Characters. For where-ever we can diſcover the leaſt Footſteps of Plays, and where Learning ever flouriſh'd in any tolerable degree, I think we may trace them plainly enough, we ſhall certainly find all, or at leaſt moſt of the foremention'd Characters, very frequently made uſe of. Indeed, 'tis a Liberty not to be deny'd, at leaſt if you'll give any Credit to the famous *Corneille,* who for near ſixty Years together ſupply'd the *French* Stage with many admirable Plays, and who did himſelf make uſe of that Liberty with as much Caution, Modeſty, and Reſervedneſs, as any Poet could poſſibly do. He, ſpeaking of the Manners of a Dramatick Poem, tells us that *Ariſtotle* requir'd four Things as

neceſ-

necessary to render them compleat. The
first of which was, that they should be
Good; by which Word Good, some of
his Interpreters were apt to believe, that
they ought to be strictly Virtuous. But
that Sense of the Word *Corneille* very

Theatre de
Corn. Tom.
1. Disc. du
Poeme
Dramat. *p.*
15.

plainly rejects, saying, *Je ne puis com-
prendre, comment on a voulu entendre,
par ce Mot de bonnes, qu'il faut qu'elles
soient Verteueuses. La plus part des
Poems, tant anciens, que modernes, de-
meureroient en un pitayable ètat; si l'on
en retranchoiet, tout ce qu'il s'y rencontre
de Personages mechans, ou vitieux, ou ta-
chez de quelque foibless, qui s'accord mal
avec la Vertu.* The same *Corneille* comes
up yet closer to the Point in hand, in
another Place, where he tells us there
had been several Invectives then newly
publish'd against the Stage; to all which
he returns little more than this, *La Co-*

Theatre de
Corn. Tom.
4. Examen.
d'Attila.

*medie est assez justifiée, par cette celebre
traduction de la moietie de celles, de Terence, que des personnes d'une pieté exem-
plaire, & rigid, ont donnèe au Public; &
ne l'auroient jamais fait, si elles n'eussent
juge, qu'on peut innocement mettre sur la
scene, de filles engrossées par leurs Amants,
& des Marchands d'esclaves a prostiteur.*
Thus we see that several Persons in *France*,
of an exemplary and rigid Piety, Tran-
slated

flated and Publifh'd fome of *Terence* his Comedies; and we may thereupon very well Conclude with *Corneille,* that they would never have done it, had they not been of the Opinion, that vicious Characters might very innocently be brought upon the Stage.

Tho' what has been already faid, may be abundantly enough to fatisfie any indifferent Perfon, yet becaufe every Days Experience teaches us, that a Prejudice is ever much cafier taken up at firft, than afterwards remov'd, I fhall proceed farther to fhew you what the Poet may do, by what the Hiftorian frequently does. For, fince both the one and the other pretend to one and the fame end, for my part, I can't fee any reafon why all the Means conducing to that End fhould not be equally indulg'd to both. Nor can the one, I think, with any manner of Juftice lay claim to any Privilege, which the other may not as well every whit pretend to. And therefore, if the Hiftorian may fafely and innocently give a Place in his Works, to the laft hellifh Speech of the expiring Apoftate *Julian, Vicifti tandem Galilæe Vicifti.* ; Why may not the Poet as fafely, and as innocently, make the fame *Julian* die on the Stage, with the fame Words in his Mouth; or

E 3   any

any other feign'd Person as he, with the like. But what! Is not the Historian then strictly ty'd up to the Truth, and may he not, on that account, pretend to some Advantage over the Poet? who certainly is not. No, by no means: For tho' I readily grant, that the Historian is so far confin'd to the Truth, as that he must leave nothing behind him on Record as such, but what is strictly true; yet he lyes under no Obligation, that I know of, of taking notice of all Truths. Nay, it is not properly his Business to meddle with any but such as are, some way or other, necessary to the clear and better Understanding of the most remarkable Transactions of those Times he pretends to write of. All other Truths, especially such as may give any Offence to the Reader, being wholly foreign to his purpose. And here I dare Appeal to Mr. *Collier* himself, whether these last Words of *Julian* be not yet more grating to the Ear of a good Christian, than any thing he ever meet with in the very lewdest of all our Plays. Let us therefore see what Necessity there was of the Historian's taking notice of them. What necessary Piece of Knowledge did he thereby convey down to succeeding Ages? Or what new Light did they lend to any dark or obscure Pas-

fage in his Hiftory? Might we not otherwife have known, that *Julian* had Apo-
ftatiz'd from the Faith? that he defign'd
the utter Extirpation of the Chriftian Religion? And had not that been enough to
have given Pofterity a right Notion of
the Man? Certainly it had; and if fo,
then what can the Hiftorian fay for himfelf by way of Excufe, which the Poet
may not urge with as good Succefs as he.
Indeed Plays are but fhorter Hiftories,
nor are they e'er the lefs Inftructive, for
being, as many of them are, meer Fictions. For we know, that many of the
wifeft Men in all Ages, have made choice
of Fables, as the moft familiar, eafie and
effectual way of Inftruction. And Sir *William D'Avenant,* one of our beft Poets,
has very plainly and ingenioufly deliver'd his Opinion of them, in his Survey
of *Aftragon's* Study, where paffing by
fome of the old Philofophers careflefly
enough, he proceeds thus:

Near them are grave dull Moralifts,   Gondibert
       (who give   Cant. 5. p.
Counfel to fuch, as ftill in publick dwell,   177.
At Sea in Courts, and Camps, and Ci-
       (ties live,
And fcorn Experience from their pra-
       (ctis'd Cell.
             Æfop

Æsop with these stands high, and they
                                    (below,
His pleasant Wisdom mocks their Gra-
                                    (vity,
Who Virtue like a tedious Matron shew,
He dresses Nature to invite the Eye.

High Skill their Ethicks seem, whilst
                              (he stoops down,
To make the People wise; their learned
                                    (Pride
Makes all obscure, that we may prize
                                    (Gown;
With Ease he teaches what with Pain
                                    (they hide.

But that which must put an end to all
Disputes, concerning the Lawfulness and
Usefulness of Fiction, is the Example of
our Ever-Blessed Saviour himself; who,
in the Propagation of his most Holy Doctrine, made frequent use of Parables,
which in the Opinion of the Learned,
were all meer Fictions: And so much for
that.

I shall now proceed to the Proof of my
third and last Particular; That vicious
Characters not only may, but many times
ought to be brought upon the Stage.
Now, if the true and native Beauty of
Virtue

Virtue can be no way set off so much to advantage, or so easily comprehended as when plac'd in a true Light, and near its contrary Vice; the Deformity of which, not only adds a new Lustre to her Charms, but scares too the indifferent Pretender into her Embraces; insomuch that delighted on the one hand, and frighted on the other, no Man of any tolerable Sense can never miscarry in his Choice; then certainly, vicious Characters may be of admirable use on the Stage, as the most effectual and ready Means to recommend Virtue to an Audience. Sir *Philip Sidney,* that great Ornament of the Age he liv'd in, is clearly of that Opinion. "Comedy, says he, is an Imitation of the common Errors of our Life, which the Poet represents in the most ridiculous and scornful sort that may be. Now as in Geometry the Oblique must be known as well as the Right, and in Arithmetick the Odd as well as the Even; so in the Actions of our Life, who seeth not the Filthiness of Evil, wanteth a great Foil to perceive the Beauty of Virtue. So that the right use of Comedy will, I think, by no body be blam'd; and much less of the high and excellent Tragedy, that openeth the greatest Wounds, and sheweth forth the "Ulcers

Defence of Poetry.

" Ulcers that are cover'd with Tiffue,
" that maketh Kings fear to be Tyrants,
" and Tyrants manifeft their tyrannical
" Humours, that with ftirring the Effects
" of Admiration, and Commiferation,
" teacheth the Uncertainty of this World,
" and upon how weak Foundations
" gilden Roofs are builded, that maketh us
" know that *Qui Sceptra fævus duro im-*
" *perio regit, timet timentes, metus in*
" *Authorem redit.* Thus far Sir *Philip
Sidney,* whofe Opinion in the Cafe is fo
confiderable, that I fhould never have
thought of adding any thing more to it,
but that there is yet one Gentleman's Authority that offers it felf, and to which
Mr. *Collier* perhaps may be apt to pay a
greater Deference ; I mean, his own.
For he indeed has given himfelf fome
trouble, tho' why or wherefore, I muft
confefs, I cannot very well tell, to prove
Inftruction, and not Diverfion, to be the
Main and Principal End of Plays. Now
if that be fo, then what can be more Inftructive than thofe Examples the Stage
may every Day produce, of great and illuftrious Perfons, adorn'd with many
rare and admirable Virtues ; all which
Virtues have been eclipfed, fhaded, nay
totally obfcur'd by fome one black, prevailing Vice? The fatal Confequences of
which

which, duly reprefented on the Stage,
cannot but prove a moft effectual Perfua-
five to Virtue. Thus would we from
the great Folly and Danger of Atheifm,
Irreligion, or Apoftafie, endeavour to recommend Virtue, Piety and Goodnefs
to the World; how could we better do
it, than from the Example of a *Julian*?
Who, tho' a Prince of as great Hopes
as ever mounted the Imperial Throne,
tho'. Mafter of many bright and fhining
Virtues; tho' Courteous, Liberal, Wife
and Valiant; all royal, lovely, and en-
dearing Qualities; yet after that one horrid Act of his Apoftafie, how was he defpis'd and fcorn'd of all good Men? How
odious was his Life, and how remarkable
his Death? Again, would we from the Sin,
the uneafie Cares and criminal Toils of
a reftlefs and unfatiable Ambition, frame
a prevailing Argument, to perfuade the
World to Eafe and Innocence, thofe happy Fruits of a fedate and quiet Temper;
how could we better do it, than from the
dreadful Example of our *Richard* the
Third? Who after fo many Villanies, fo
many execrable Murders, committed in
his way to a Crown, was by the Divine
Providence forc'd, e'er that Crown was
yet well fettled on his Head, to leave
both that and his lifelefs Carkafs in the
same

same bloody Field; the one to be worn
by the Victorious *Richmond,* the other
to be derided, mock'd and abus'd by all
the World. But once more; Would we
recommend Love and Mercy, Pity and
Compassion to the World; would we set
all the Blemishes of a rough and cruel Nature, in such a Light as would be sure
to render it most odious. How could we
better do it, than from the Example of
our *Henry* the Eighth? Of whom Sir *Wal-
ter Raleigh* sticks not to say, "That if all
"the Pictures and Patterns of a merciless
"Prince were lost in the World, they
"might all again be painted to the Life,
"out of the Story of that King. For
"how many Wives, says the same Au-
"thor, did he cut off; what causeless,
"and cruel Wars did he make upon his
"own Nephew *James* the Fifth; what
"Laws and Wills did he devise to esta-
"blish the Kingdom in his own Issue,
"using his sharpest Weapons to cut off
"and cut down those Branches, which
"sprang from the same Root that himself
"did; and yet in the End, it pleas'd God
"to take away all his own without In-
"crease; tho' for themselves, in their se-
"veral Kinds, all Princes of eminent
"Virtue. Nor indeed was he himself
wholly destitute of all Royal Qualities,

*Pref. to his
Hist. of the
World.*

for

for setting aside that one great Blemish of his Reign, his Cruelty; he was otherwise a Learned, Wise, Magnanimous and Couragious Prince. But all his real Accomplishments were all lost, all drown'd in that prodigious Sea of Blood his Cruelty had spilt.

And now, I hope, I have in some measure satisfy'd every unprejudic'd Reaner, that vicious Characters not only may, but ought to be brought upon the Stage, as useful and instructive. I must confess, that Mr. *Collier* has no where, that I know of, absolutely banish'd all such Characters. Tho' when he tells us, that no Stage-Discipline can atone for the Misrepresentation of any thing, either smutty or prophane, he very plainly cuts off so many from the Stage, that he leaves the Poets but very few or none at all to practise upon: And so has here, once more, given us a very smart touch of his admirable Faculty of Reforming so many great and useful Characters out of doors, as, added to those I have already taken notice of, would be abundantly enough to silence the Stage for ever.

But how then? Must all vicious Characters be indifferently admitted on the Stage? and under that Pretence, shall our Poets dare wanton with Sin, and at their

their Pleasure vent their own filthy, nau-
seous Conceptions? Shall the Comedian,
in the Person of a Pimp, a Whore, or a
Bawd, fly out into all the grossest Extravagances of Smut, and ransack the
very Stews for Language to adorn his
Characters? Or shall the Tragick Poet,
under the Shelter of an irreligious, or
atheistical Person, fly presently into the
Face of Heav'n, defie his Maker, prophane his most holy Name, blaspheme at
any rate; and all this under the Protection of our Stage-Discipline? By no means:
Many things, lawful enough in themselves, may be so circumstanc'd as to
become unlawful, nay sinful, and that in
a very high degree. Besides, every thing
that may be lawful, may not be expedi-
ent, may not be decent; and I think our
Poets oblig'd to observe all the Rules of
Decency, that are not destructive of their
Art. Here therefore, tho' perhaps it
may be absolutely impossible to assign
any such certain Limits in this Case, but
that something must still be left to the
Discretion of the Poet, whose Conscience alone can properly condemn or ac-
quit him in this Particular: Yet to clear
my own Meaning, and to render what I
have been hitherto aiming at yet more
plain and more intellible to every indifferent

rent Reader, I fhall venture to propofe
fome fuch Bounds to our Poets, as if
°once admitted, may, in my poor Opinion, not only contribute very much to a
right and rational Reformation of our
Stage, but bring our Plays to the very
higheft Perfection they have ever yet attain'd, or in their own Nature are capable of; which I take to be the Duty of
every fair Reformer, let the Thing reform'd be what it will. Now our Poets,
as our Plays, being of two very different
Sorts, which cannot both poffibly fall
under one and the fame Rule, to avoid
Confufion, I fhall confider them feveral-
ly. Firft then for the Comick Poet:
Since a great part of his Bufinefs is Mirth
and Jollity, he ought not certainly to
fhew any thing on the Stage, that may
create a Horror in the Spectators. No
Vices, but fuch as the Audience may
fafely laugh at, and all Offenders in the
like kind be probably laugh'd out of. He
has nothing at all to do with any thing
extreamly lewd, or in the leaft prophane:
Nothing either Atheiftical, or Irreligious,
fhould fall from his Pen under any pretence of Character whatfoever; much lefs
fhould he offer at any thing of that nature, when even that Pretence is wanting.
Thefe two laft are both fuch Faults, as,

in

in my Opinion, he ought very carefully to avoid; the one, as he's a Poet; the other, as he's a Christian. But above all, he must not pretend to meddle with any thing that is either Sacred in it self, or by Custom appropriated to sacred Uses. No Story, no Phrase, no Expression whatsoever in the Bible, may be repeated, or so much as alluded to, without Sin. The Holy Bible is sacred, in every the minutest Part of it; 'tis that glorious Charter, by which alone we can ever hope to be invested in all the Privileges of the New *Jerusalem*; the sacred Record of our great God's gracious Promises to Mankind; that bless'd Fountain of pure, living Water, whence we draw all our sweetest Hopes of Life, and Everlasting Happiness. And shall a Poet then dare to prophane, to ridicule this Bible, or any the least Part of it? No certainly; the dismal Consequences of such an Impiety are too terrible, and too certain. There is no trifling, no jesting, with a Text of Scripture, but what will infallibly end in sad and woful earnest: No such horrid and preposterous Mirth, but what must terminate, without God's intervening Mercy on Repentance, in weeping, wailing, and gnashing of Teeth. But now, tho' our Poet must by no means venture

venture on Crimes of fo vaft, and fo prodigious a Bulk, that no Punifhment, but that of Hell it felf, can bear any the leaft Proportion to them; yet there are fome certain Vices, or rather feeming Vices, which Mr. *Collier* however will not allow of, fuch as Smut, and thofe By-Words, which he calls Oaths, which properly enough may, and very naturally do fall under the Cognizance of the Comick Poet.

As for Smut, I fhall only fay this, that it ought never to be fpoken out of Character, and when in Character, it muft not be too grofs, either in the Terms, or in the Senfe: And then I think the Poet may be fafe enough. For when Smut, to ufe the common Phrafe of the Vulgar, is handfomly wrapt up in clean Linnen, I can fee no great Danger in it: much lefs can I blame the Ufe of a double *Entendre,* that is eafie and natural, tho' it fhould fometimes appear in good civil Company. And fo let that pafs.

As for difguis'd Oaths, which in reality are nothing elfe, but fome certain By-Words, altogether infignificant in themfelves; and taken up, for the moft part, by fome good People only to avoid fwearing: I can by no means imagine, why the Comick Poet may not freely make

F   what

what ufe of them he pleafes. For, fhall
thofe By-Words be thought finful, that
were firft brought up only to avoid Sin?
Or becaufe perhaps they retain fome few
of the fame Letters, nay fome fmall Matter, it may be, of the fame Twang too
with fome Oaths, muft they prefently be
cenfur'd as fuch? Shall not the common
Practice of fo many Perfons of known
Probity, Virtue, and Honour, as very
frequently make ufe of them in the
World, rather juftifie their Ufe too on
the Stage? Mr. *Collier* does not deny, but
that they are very often us'd in common
Converfation, yet will by no means allow
that to be any Argument of their Innocence. For when the Vindicator offers
Reply to it as fuch, he prefently cries out, *What*
the Short *means he to infift fo much upon Prece-*
Vind. of *dent? Does Cuftom juftifie a Fault? Is*
the *Relapfe* *Sin improv'd into Privilege? And can a*
p. 101. *Man fwear by Common Law?* Very fmart,
very witty indeed! And yet when the
Flafh and Noife is over, and we have
wip'd up our Eyes a little, I doubt not
but we may eafily fee through the notorious Sophiftry of thofe invidious Que-
ftions. For in the Cafe before us, where
is the Fault? where is the Sin? where is
the Swearing? We have Mr. *Collier's*
Word indeed, that thofe filly, infignificant

cant By-Words are Oaths, and confequently finful. But then have we not,
at the fame time, the Opinion of the
greateft Part of the World, declar'd and
made manifeft by their Practice, that
they are not fo? For certainly, no good
Men will countenance, or incourage, much
lefs themfelves practife, any thing they
think to be either evil, or finful ; and
yet, that a great many very good Men
do often ufe fuch By-Words, no body
of any Experience in the World, I think,
can deny. And therefore notwithftanding all the mighty Noife of Mr. *Collier's*
fatyrical Squibs, and Crackers, with
which he hop'd to furprize fome, fright
others, and for a time, it may be, con-
found moft of his Readers; yet it will,
at laft, appear plainly enough to any con-
fidering Perfon, that when we infift fo
much on the common Practice of good
Men, 'tis not meerly their Practice we rely upon, but their Judgment; which
Judgment of theirs, may very reafonably
be thought of Weight enough to determine, in a dubious Cafe, whether fuch
or fuch a thing be finful or no; tho' their
Practice, where the Cafe is plain, can by
no means be enough to juftifie our Sin-
ning. And fo I fhall leave the Comick
Poet to ufe his own Difcretion in this,

or

or any other the like Cafe, that may arife.
Tho', I think, I may venture to fay this
farther, in general, that as long as he
pretends to no other Liberties in Converfation on the Stage, than what are
frequently affum'd, and that without
Blame too, by Perfons of known Virtue and Integrity, of the fame Quality
in the World; he need not apprehend
the Cenfure of any Reformer whatfoe-
ever.

For that Reformer certainly is nice, and
ftrict enough, that requires fo much; and
he that pretends to more, is unreafonable. He feeks, in all probability, but
an occafion of quarrelling, and the Ruin,
rather than the Reformation of the Stage.
And fo much for the Comedian.

Now for the Tragick Poet; his chief
End is certainly Inftruction. It is not
therefore his Bufinefs to laugh at, but to
punifh Vice; and that too, even in Kings
and Princes: He, as he's not confin'd in
his Punifhments, fo neither is he any
way limited in the Choice of his Characters; which muft ever be great, illuftrious, and remarkable, either for their
Virtues, or their Vices: 'Tis no great
matter which, fince fome very eminent
Characters of either Kind may be equally inftructive; unlefs perhaps you'll allow,

low, that the Vicious may challenge some
Advantage over the other, on this one
Account; that Men are oftner frighted
from Evil, than tempted or allur'd to
Good. But now, tho' our Tragick Poet may not be limited in the Choice of
his Characters, yet in the Management
of them he must. Thus, tho' he may
innocently enough bring an Atheist, or
an Apostate, on the Stage; yet is he by
no means oblig'd to let either of them
run to the end of their Line, the very
utmost Extent of his Character, or to
fill their Mouths with nothing else but
lewd, atheistical, irreligious Rants, and
those the grossest too in their Kind that
the most debauch'd Fancy can suggest.
No: Some bold Touches indeed, in such
a Case, there must be, here and there
scatter'd with Discretion; enough to set
those Characters in a true Light, and
give the Spectators a right Notion of the
Persons represented, and no more: Nay,
even those Touches too should be carefully, nicely, and artificially manag'd: In
a word, they should be just like the fi-
nishing Strokes of a skilful Painter, which
tho' but few, and those too, in all Appearance, but carelessly laid on, do yet
give the greatest Life and Likeness to a
Picture. To make short work therefore
F 3   with

with the Tragick Poet, let him but obferve thefe few Cautions in the Management of all vicious Characters, and ftick
clofe to his Stage-Difcipline, and then, I
think, he cannot well give Offence to
any reafonable or unprejudic'd Perfon.
Mr. *Collier* indeed will not allow of any
the leaft Prophanefs on the Stage, under
any Pretence of Character or Difcipline
whatfoever. And therefore, in pure Kind-
nefs, no doubt of it, to his very particular Friends the Stage-Poets, he tells 'em
how they may bring any wicked Perfon,
as an Atheift, or fo, on the Stage, nay
and punifh him too for his Wickednefs,
and yet not one lewd, prophane, or atheiftical Word, or any thing tending that
way, to be heard all the while. *Partu-*
riunt Montes——To fay a Man has been
prophane, in general, and then to punifh
him, is fomewhat intelligible; to make
him an Example without Inftance, or Par-
ticularity, is a fafe way of Dramatick
Juftice. Very pretty Stuff this! He has
hitherto taken a great deal of Pains to
render the Stage odious, and now he is
trying what he can do, towards the making of it ridiculous: For what in nature
can be more ridiculous, than this Piece
of Dramatick Juftice of his? How is it
poffible to diftinguifh the Character of an
Atheift,

Reply to Mr. Cong. Amend. p. 16.

Atheiſt, from that of a Man of Piety and Religion, but by ſomething in his Diſcourſe, plainly inconſiſtent with either? Or ſhall we fix a Paper on his Forehead, that ſhall give the Lie to his Tongue, and in ſpite of all outward Appearance, declare him a very Atheiſt in his Heart? This indeed is one way of ſhewing the Monſter, but withal a very ſcurvy one at the beſt; and therefore Mr. *Collier,* as you ſee, has found out another; he muſt have an ill Name given him, it muſt be ſaid by ſome body, that ſomewhere, or at ſome time or other, he had been prophane in his Diſcourſe; and then there's no more to be done, but away with him preſently to Execution. And that is making an Example, without Inſtance or Particularity; in plain *Engliſh,* judging without Proceſs, and condemning without Proof; which is certainly the greateſt Injuſtice imaginable. And how then dares Mr. *Collier* recommend it to the Play-houſe? Since, according to his Doctrine, let but any Vice appear upon the Stage, and immediately all the World muſt fall in Love with it, nay run downright mad after it, and that too, tho' it be repreſented in the moſt ugly Shape, and under all the diſcouraging Circumſtances, the Wit of Man can invent. For

F 4   who

who then shall secure us, that his Thea-
tral Piece of Justice, shall not in time become National? Or that it may not, hereafter, be many an honest Man's hard For-
tune, to be condemn'd by Report, and
hang'd by Hearsay? These Fears, I must
confess, are something remote, and consequently not very reasonable; and yet
neither more remote, nor less reasonable,
than most of those Mr. *Collier* pretends
to labour under, almost in every Page of
his celebrated *View*. And indeed, they
there stand him in such notable stead,
that I dare boldly affirm, were they once
fairly remov'd, there would not, in his
whole Book, be left so much as the bare
Shadow of an Argument against a well-
regulated Stage. For what was it, think
you, that inspir'd him with this eminent
Piece of Justice? What set him upon
making of Examples, without Instance
or Particularity, but his nice and unreasonable Fears? They are, indeed, the
perpetual Burthen of his Song. Thus,
he has no sooner very kindly recommend-
ed his new Piece of comfortable Justice
to his good Friends the Stage-Poets, but
he presently falls into a long and violent
Haranguing; that is, he very naturally
passes from one sort of trifling to another;
and both alike founded on those Frights
and

and Fears I have been fpeaking of. It
may not therefore be much amifs, to enquire a little more particularly here, of
what Nature thofe his Fears may be, and
what juft Grounds he may have for them.
In the firft place, I fuppofe, he pretends
that nothing either fmutty, or prophane,
can be fpoken on the Stage, without Sin
either in the Poet, in the Player, or perhaps in both. But I think I have already
fufficiently clear'd that Scruple, under his
firft Particular of the Prophanefs charg'd
on the Stage, Swearing and Curfing. To
what therefore I have either there, or
elfewhere faid on this Subject, I fhall only add this one thing more ; that if the
bare repeating of any thing prophane be
a Sin, then many reverend, pious, and
learned Men may, nay do, and muft fin
in anfwering Lewd, Atheiftical, or Heretical Books; which they cannot do to a-
ny purpofe, without repeating, or, which
is all one, quoting a great deal of their
Ribaldry. Thus we fee, Mr. *Collier,*
having very well obferv'd the great Impiety of fome of our modern Poets, and
not without Reafon, thinking himfelf in
Duty bound to chaftife them for their
Lewdnefs; the more effectually to expofe them, and terrifie others from tread-
ing in their Steps, has furnifh'd us with
fuch

such a Collection of lewd, blasphemous, and atheistical Stuff, as few Books extant can parallel, and nothing, I am confident, can ever atone for, but the Design with which he did it. Here then, by the by, I desire to know why the same good Design shall not atone for the same Attempt in our Poets? What do they pretend to more, than he has actually done; Nay they dare not pretend to so much. For Mr. *Collier,* we see, flies at all; the more daring, the more horrid the Expressions are, the fitter he thinks them for his purpose: Whereas our Poets are stinted, confin'd to the Choice of that which may be the least offensive. But to all this it may perhaps be return'd, that Mr. *Collier* has a Call to what he does of that Nature; which the Poet cannot pretend to. And why not? I must confess indeed, that he has no extraordinary Call to the Functions of Preaching, and Praying; but yet a Call he has, an ordinary Call, the common Call of every Christian, by virtue of which he is in Duty bound to guide, help, and assist, to advise, exhort, and admonish, tho' not to comptrol and punish his Christian Brother. But to return to the Point in hand.

Tho'

Tho' the Reprefentation of any thing lewd, or prophane, may not in it felf be finful, yet furely it may, nay in all probability it muft be dangerous; as that which may contribute very much towards the debauching of the lefs fteady, and more youthful Part of an Audience. And this indeed is what he, all along, pretends to be moft afraid of. *The Play-house often fpreads thofe Vices it reprefents, and the Humour of the Town is learn'd by fhewing it.*   How! Are thofe Vices then that our Poets reprefent on the Stage the Humour of the Town? Certainly Mr. *Collier* was in great Hafte, when he let that Truth flip from his Pen, which plainly contradicts what he has very confidently afferted, not only in his Preface, but more than once too in his *View, viz.* That it was the Stage that had poifon'd the Town; whereas by what he here fays, we muft conclude that it was the Town rather that debauch'd the Stage. But let that pafs: Let us now fee what great Danger there may be in a fair and regular Reprefentation of any thing vicious or prophane on the Stage; and what juft Reafon Mr. *Collier* may have, for his extraordinary Fears in that Particular. One would think that a due Obfervation of our Stage-Difcipline, fhould

Reply to Mr. *Cong.* Amend. *p.* 16.

should be enough to prevent all manner of Danger; and that Vice, set forth in all its truest Colours, represented in an ugly, hideous, terrifying Shape; all a-long censur'd, and condemn'd as odious, and at last severely punish'd as criminal and sinful, should have but few Charms for the Spectators; especially whilst Virtue, at the same time, appears in all her native Splendor, heighten'd by all the additional Ornaments that Wit and Poetry can invent, to render her, if possible, yet more lovely. But alas! All this signifies just nothing to Mr. *Collier,* let the Poet represent Virtue never so charming, let him render Vice never so deform'd, let him say what he will for the one, or what he can against the other, yet so strangely prone must we be thought to Evil, that in spight of Education, Sense, Reason, or Religion, our Youth must needs reject Virtue, and run after Vice, slight Heaven, and fall in Love with Hell and Damnation; and all this, as the *French* express themselves, *de gaité de Cœur,* without any manner of Temptation, Hope, or Prospect, either of Pleasure, Praise or Profit: Nay, and at that very nick of time too, when the Poet is actually employing all his Skill, all his Art, to divert and dissuade them from it.

Well:

Well: Since Mr. *Collier* will needs have it so, I will allow there may possibly be some few such Madmen in the World. But what of all that! almost every Day's sad Experience tells us there are some Wretches so desperately wicked and foolish, that rather than not go to Hell, they will make use of Sword, Pistol, or Blunderbuss, as their securest Pass-port thither. And shall we therefore deny the Use of those necessary Arms to others, only because they were pleas'd to abuse them to their own Destruction? Here let us suppose a friendly Light placed high, near the Sea-Coast, to shew the Danger of some neighbouring Rock; what would Mr. *Collier* think of those Sailors, that should not only slight the charitable Warning, but obstinately make use even of that very Light to guide and direct them to their own Ruin? Or, to illustrate the matter by a more familiar Instance, let us, if you please, for once suppose our Author, in a dark Winter's Evening, walking the *London* Streets, should take the Opportunity of those Lights, then and there expos'd for the common Benefit of Mankind, to level his Nose more directly against a Post. Certainly we should have Reason enough

to

to wonder at the extravagant Fancy, and I dare fay, he would hardly have the Confidence to petition my Lord Mayor againft thofe Lights, only becaufe 'twas his Pleafure, to the real Damage of his Nofe, and no great Commendation of his Underftanding, fo miferably to per-vert the Ufe of them. But enough of this: I fhall only obferve from hence, that Mr. *Collier*, from thefe his unreafonable Fears, does not only reflect very feverely on the Morals of his Country-men, but on their Intellectuals too.

The famous *Corneille* gives us a very different Character of the *French*. He reprefents them as fuch Lovers of Virtue, and Haters of Vice, that they cannot with any Patience endure to fee the one any way deprefs'd, or the other in the leaft exalted on the Stage. And indeed, to that commendable Humour of theirs it is, that he afcribes the Neceffity the *French* Poets lye under, of obferving a moft ftrict Stage-Difcipline: Which Difcipline, he will not allow to be any otherwife a con-ftant Rule of their Art. *En effet,* fays he, *il eft certain, que nous ne fcaurious voir un honefte, homme fur notre Theatre, fans luy fouhaiter de la profperité, & nous fafcher de fes infortunes. Cela fait, que*

Theatre de Corn.Tom. 1. Difc. du Poeme Dramati-que *p.* 23.

que quand il en demeure accablè, nous sor-
tons avec chagrin, & remportons une es-
pecè d'indignation contre l'Auteur, & les
Acteurs mais quand l'erenement remplit
nos souhaits, & que la vertue y est cou-
ronnée; nous sortons avec plein joye, &
remportons une entiere satisfaction & de
l'ouvrage, & de ceux qui l'ont representé.
Le succes de la vertu, en depit des tra-
verses, & de perils; nous excite a l'am-
brasser, & les succes funeste du Crime, ou
de l'injustice, est capable de nous en aug-
menter l'horreur naturelle, par l'apprehen-
sion d'une pareile malheur. Thus we see
he represents his Country-Men always
siding with Virtue, and discountenancing
of Vice: Nay, he tells you, that they
are apt to Court the very Miseries of the
one; whereas the most dreadful Misfor-
tunes of the other do but encrease their
natural Aversion for it. It is a very difficult thing, to pretend to encounter with
other Peoples Fears, and absolutely impossible to overcome them, if they themselves at the same time are resolv'd, right or
wrong, to hug, cherish, and defend them.
There may be perhaps some People in
the World, so unreasonable shall I say,
or uncharitable rather, as to tax Mr. *Col-*
lier with Rashness at least, if not with a
downright evil Design, in publishing his
View;

View; and to fear that by his induftri-
ous Collection of fo much Blafphemous
and Atheiftical Ribaldry, he may have
done more Harm, than all the reft of
his Book is like to do Good. They
may pretend indeed, that he has taken a
great deal of unneceffary Pains to rake
together a vaft heap of Rubbiſh, which
before lay fo difpers'd in fmaller Parcels, as
not to be eafily difcover'd : And therefore neither fo offenfive to good Men,
nor fo dangerous to the Bad, as it may
now prove in the Lump, where 'tis more
eafie to be come at, more charming for
its variety, and every way more beautiful in the Eyes of Fools and Madmen.
All this, I fay, may poffibly be objected
againft his *View*; and how, I pray, will
Mr. *Collier* evade the Charge? Why, I
doubt not but he will, in the firft place,
be apt to make himfelf merry with thofe
Gentlemen and their Fears; and beftow
a Satyrical Jerk or two upon them for
their Folly; and then, as he very well
may, return them fuch an Anfwer as
may be full and fatisfactory to any unprejudic'd rational Man.   Well then, I
fuppofe all this already done.   But what
does it fignifie? The Gentlemen are not
only unreafonable, but obftinate too in
their Fears; notwithftanding all that he
can

can fay, in fpite of all Senfe, or Reafon,
they ftill blunder on; and pretending to
be fcar'd almoft out of their Wits, with
the Apprehenfions of the fad Confequences attending fuch a dangerous Piece,
ftill cry out louder and louder, Away
with this infamous Collection, *It is not
to be endured, no Pretence whatever can*
excufe, or make it tolerable. 'Tis grating
to Chriftian Ears, difhonourable to the
Majefty of God, and dangerous in the Ex-
ample. It tends to no Point, unlefs it
be to wear off the Horrour of the Practice,
to weaken the Force of Confcience, and to
teach the Language of the Damn'd. Here
now is a great Torrent of Rhetorick indeed, tho' but little Reafon; but how
can he help himfelf, if they will perfift
in the Humour of topping the one upon
him, for the other? For my part, I know
of no Remedy but Patience, and a modeft
Appeal to the more equal Judgment of
the indifferent and impartial Reader. And
fo without any more Ceremony, I pafs
on to his next Chapter, which appears
under the Title of

View, p.
96.

G　　　　*The*

The Clergy abus'd by the Stage.

I shall have but little to say under this one Head, as perfectly agreeing, in this at least, with Mr. *Collier*, that the Clergy ought by no means to be abus'd, or ridicul'd on the Stage. They are the Representatives of our great and glorious God; they are the Reverend Fathers of the Church, appointed and ordain'd to watch over us their Children, for our Good even in this World, and our eternal Welfare in the next: They are the Sacred Dispensers of the most High and Holy Mysteries of Religion. And yet they are but Men, subject to Passions and to Errors. But then ought we not much rather to hide, than to expose their Faults? Ought we not rather to conceal their Infirmities, if not out of Civility, if not out of Common Charity, yet out of Respect at least, to that great God whose Ministers they are? Yes certainly; and I do not at all doubt, but that God, who is a jealous God, and of nothing more jealous than of his Honour, will in his own due time severely punish all those Indignities, all those Affronts put upon them, as levell'd against himself, and consequently derogatory

gatory in the higheſt Degree, from his
infinite Majeſty. The firſt thing therefore, that I ſhall take notice of under this
Head, is a pleaſant Remark our Author
has been pleas'd to make, on a certain Paſſage in *OEdipus* ; of which he ſeems ſo
very fond, that tho' it did not at all lye
in his way, yet according to a rambling
ſort of a Humour, very prevalent with
him, thro' the whole courſe of his *View*,
he makes nothing of ſtepping aſide to
fetch it in, and ſo here we have it, as little perhaps to my Purpoſe as 'twas to his.
However, let us now ſee, whether it may
be worth the Pains we have both taken
about it. When *Ægean* brought the
News of King *Polybus's* Death, *OEdipus* was wonderfully ſurpriz'd with the
Relation.

OEdip *O all ye Pow'rs ! Is't poſſible ?* OEdipus,
        (What Dead !   p. 48.

And why not ? ſays our Author, *Was*   View, p.
the Man Invulnerable or Immortal ? No- 100.
thing of that : He was only fourſcore and
ten Years old, that was his main Securi-
ty, and if you'll believe the Poet, He fell
like Autumn Fruit, that mellow'd long,
even wonder'd at becauſe dropp'd no
ſooner.

And

And which is more, Œdipus *muſt needs be acquainted with his Age, having ſpent the greateſt part of his time with him at* Corinth.

Very well: But is he ſure he does not wrong the Poet in all this, nor miſrepreſent his Meaning. Let us ſee a little: The Story of *OEdipus* runs thus; *OEdipus,* quickly after his Birth expos'd by his Mother to be ſlain, was ſav'd and convey'd to *Corinth,* where King *Polybus,* having no Children by his Queen *Merope,* and taken with the Beauty of the Infant, reſolves to impoſe him on his People as his own Child, and breed him up as Heir to his Crown. Some Years after, *OEdipus* being upbraided as a Fondling, by ſomebody that had, it ſeems, got ſome light into the Secret, immediately quits *Corinth,* with a deſign to enquire farther into the Matter; and accordingly conſults the Oracle at *Delphos,* and receives this Anſwer.

Fly, Wretch, whom Fate has doom'd thy
　　　　(Father's Blood to ſpill,
And with prepoſtrous Births thy Mo-
　　　　(ther's Womb to fill.

OEdipus amaz'd, and ſtruck with Horrour at ſo ſtrange an Anſwer, reſolves
　　　　　　　　　　　never

never to return to *Corinth* 'till after the Death of *Polybus* and *Merope*, whom he still thought his Parents. He therefore ranges the wide World, and roams about, 'till at last coming to *Thebes*, and by the *Thebans* chosen to be their King, thither *Ægeon* brings him the welcome News of *Polybus*'s Death; at which he presently falls into strange and unusual Raptures of Surprize and Joy.

And now pray where's the Jest of all this? The Gods had assur'd *OEdipus*, a Prince of eminent Piety and Virtue, that by his Hand *Polybus* should fall; what wonder then, that by his Death *OEdipus* should be surpriz'd to find, either those Gods mistaken, or the Decree of Fate it self revers'd and baffled in his Favour? Nor was it the Crime of Parricide alone with which he had been threaten'd, but that of Incest too; had he not then great Reason to fall even into an Excess of Joy and Transport, on the Belief that those same Gods, who had already secur'd him from one part of his uneasie Fears, might as well deliver him, in time, too from the other? Where is there any thing incongruous, or in the least improper in all this? If Mr. *Collier* be light-hearted, and will laugh at a Feather, who can help it. But pray observe the Ingenuity of the

Gen-

Gentleman all this while: He takes no notice at all of that Part of the Story, which alone could juftifie the Joy and Surprize which *OEdipus* fell into on that Occafion; but inftead of that, runs away with a miferable Jeft or two, drawn from View, *p.* 106, 107. the Age of *Polybus.* *The Pith of the Story,* fays he, *lyes in this Circumftance, a Prince of ninety Years was dead, and one that was wonder'd at for dying no fooner. And now why fo much Exclamation upon this Occafion ? Why muft all the Powers in Being be fummon'd in to make the News credible ? This Poffe of Interjections would have been more feafonably rais'd, if the Man had been alive.* Now to all this I fhall fay no more, but that where-ever the Pith of the Story may lye, here I am fure lyes the Malice of Mr. *Collier's* Remark, that he fhamefully and falfly reprefents the Meaning of the Poet, and impofes upon his Reader: That he manifeftly injures the one and banters the other; and fo very civily diverts himfelf at the Expences of them both.

Though we have hitherto confider'd Mr. *Collier* as a Reformer only, yet, as you may have feen, we have met with a great many Rubs, a great many bold Strokes, but little agreeing with that Character. The very Truth is, he has all
along

along befpatter'd our Poets, and bedawb'd
our Stage at an unreafonable rate; nor
does his Malice yet feem to be exhau-
fted, it rather grows and increafes upon
him. For here he very roundly tells us,
that our Poets *Aim is to deftroy Religion;* View, p.
their Preaching is againft Sermons, and 124.
their Bufinefs but Diverfion at the beft.
And a little after, fpeaking of the Clergy,
he delivers himfelf thus : *Let the Cha-*
racter be never fo well manag'd, no Chri-
ftian Prieft efpecially ought to come on
the Stage. For where the Bufinefs is an
Abufe, and the Place a Prophanation,
the Demeurnefs of the Manner is but a
poor Excufe. Very luftily laid on believe
me! But after all, what does he mean by
thefe Words? *Where the Bufinefs is an*
Abufe. Does he mean that the general
Bufinefs of the Stage, *viz.* all Plays,
are fo? That then I take to be a plain
and formal Declaration againft all Plays
whatfoever; and fo there's an End of the
Bufinefs of Reforming; or would he li-
mit and reftrain his Meaning to fuch
Plays only, as pretend to meddle with
the facred Character of a Chriftian Prieft?
And then we muft underftand him thus;
where-ever a Prieft is reprefented, tho' never fo Refpectfully, never fo Grave, never fo Serious, yet on that Account only
it

it shall be an Abuse. But then, what does he talk of the Stage? Why does he tell us a Priest must not be brought on the Stage? as if there only he were in Danger? Whereas he should have said, no Priest must on any account be brought into a Play? For whatever his Words may be, this must be his Meaning, that the Play it self, whether acted or not acted, is a Prophanation of the Priest; and how then can Mr. *Collier* have the Confidence to speak so very favourably of Mr. *Racine's Athalia?* In which *Jaiada* the High-Priest has so great a Part. *The Play,* says he, *is a very Religious Poem, 'tis upon the Matter all Sermon and Anthem, and if it were not design'd for the Stage, I have nothing to object.* Great Wits have but bad Memories; for he has already forgot, it seems, that in the Case of a Priest, the Play it self is a Prophanation, or if you had rather have it in his own Words, an Abuse. Well, but no Matter for that, on he goes couragiously, and whatever the Play may be thought, on the Account of the Priests Represented there; yet so absolutely is he resolv'd, as 'tis in a manner all Sermon and Anthem, to believe the Play-House a Prophanation of it, that he will by no means allow, that so Religious a Piece was ever

design'd

defign'd by the Author for the Stage.
He will rather fuppofe Mr. *Racine* writing for Novices, or rather downright
School-Boys: For I believe, how Magi-
fterilly foever he pretends to dictate to
Mr. *Congreve,* he would be hard put to
it to prove that there were ever any Plays
of any kind acted in Religious Houfes or
Monaftries, properly fo call'd. In the
Jefuits Colleges indeed, where they teach
Boys *Latin* and *Greek,* thofe Boys may
perhaps, at fome Solemn Times, Act a
Latin Play, or fo; tho' very rarely or
never any other. But then thofe Colleges are no Monaftries, nor does a Je-
fuit refent any thing more, than the being counted a Monk; they, in their
Hearts at leaft, defpifing the Cowl and
the Frock, as much as we can do, or as
much as any reafonable Man may fuppofe Mr. *Racine,* one of the greateft Wits
of *France,* may fcorn the low Employment of writing for fuch youngfters.
The plain Truth of the Bufinefs, after all,
is this. Tho' indeed Mr. *Collier* has Confidence to tax Mr. *Congreve* with Igno-
rance, yet is it even he himfelf, that either is, or would perhaps be contented to
be thought the Ignorant, rather than own
the *French* Cuftom of Acting the moft
Religious Plays on the Common Stage.
Yet

Yet that they have done very frequently
heretofore, and sometimes I believe do
it still, all Mr. *Corneille*'s Christian Tragedies have appear'd there, and I my self
have seen his *Polyeute* Represented with
great Applause on the Publick Theatre at
Paris. But I do not pretend that he
should take my Word in the Case, he
shall have *Moliere*'s too; and the rather,
because that he will not only satisfie him
as to the Matter of Fact, but withal convince him that the *French*, at least the
best and greatest Part of them, do not
look upon the Stage as a Prophanation
of the most Sacred Plays. It is true some
certain Bigots, in *Moliere*'s time, made a
mighty Noise upon the Occasion of his
Representing, even a *Faux Devot* upon
the Stage, pretending the Stage had nothing to do with Sacred or Religious
Matters. But *Moliere* vindicates his
Play, and obviates the most Plausible of
Tartuff. la their Objections, thus, *Je sçay bien que*
Preface. *pour reponse, ces Messeurs tachent d'insi-*
nuer, que ce n'est point au Theatre à par-
ler de ces matieres: Mais je leur demande,
avec leur permission, sur quoy ils fondent
cette belle maxime. C'est une proposition
qu'ils ne font que supposer, & qu'ils ne
prouvent en aucune façon: Et sans douté,
il ne seroit pas difficile, de leur faire voir,
que

que la Comedie, chez les Anciens a pris
son origine de la Religion ; & faisoit par-
tie de leur Mysteres ; que les Espagnols nos
voisius, ne celebrent gueres de feste, où la
Comedie ne soit meslée ; & que même par-
my nous, elle doit sa naissance aux soins
d'une Confrairie, a qui oppartient, encore
aujourd'huy, l'Hostel de Burgogne ; que
c'est un lieu qui fut donne, pour y represen-
ter les plus importans mysteres, de nôtre
essoy ; qu'on en voit encore des Comedies,
imprimiées en lettres Gothiques, tous le
nom d'un Docteur de Sarbonne, & sans
aller chercher si loin, que l'on a joué, de
nôtre temps, de Piecer Saintes de Monsieur
de Corneille, qui ont été l'admiration de
toute la France.

Thus you see that the *French* are so
far from looking on the Play-House as a
Prophanation, that they often act their
most Religious Plays on the Common
Stage; so that whatever Mr. *Collier* may
be pleas'd to fancy to the contrary, 'tis
more than probable, that even *Jaiada,*
that Play of all Sermon and Anthem,
may have taken its turn there too. But
what of all that? It makes more for his
present purpose to believe it has not; and
therefore only has not, because 'tis too good
for the Place: A very notable Reason!
A Reason that carries a Sting too in its
Tail.

Tail. For our Author, having already sufficiently expos'd thofe our Plays that are too bad; would now willingly perfuade us, there may be fome as much too good for the Stage: And then, what with thofe Plays that prophane the Play-Houfe, and thefe that may be prophan'd by it, the only way to avoid all Offence muft be, he thinks, to have no Plays at all. Mr. *Collier* has, under this Head, very handfomely difcharg'd his Duty in relation to the Clergy, and vigoroufly afferted that Honour juftly due to the whole Order. But I cannot tell for what Reafon, or by what Authority, he pretends to Entitle the Diffenting Minifters to the fame Honours, the fame Privileges with them; yet he does it, and is very angry with Mr. *Congreve* for expofing one of that Body on the Stage. A Prieft rightly Ordain'd, we all acknowledge to be the Ambaffador of God, and his Orders are his Credentials. But how a Diffenting Minifter can pretend to that Honour, or that we fhould pay him any Refpect as fuch, I cannot imagine? For he in reality is no better than an Ufurper, a meer Intruder, as having nothing to fhew, no Commiffion to juftifie his taking on him the Paftoral Charge of feeding Chrift's Flock. Notwithftanding which Mr. *Collier,*

lier, tho' himfelf of very differing Principles, has yet, it feems, a certain unac-
countable fort of Tendernefs for our Diffenting Minifters; at which fome People
have been much furpriz'd, efpecially at
the publick Profeffion he has thought fit
to make of it; tho' when all is done, 'tis
in my Opinion no fuch very ftrange Matter neither, that he, who is doing their
Drudgery for them, I mean, routing our
Poets, and overthrowing our Play-houfes, fhould make them a flight kind of
a Compliment, *en paffant,* to endear the
Obligation.   And fo having done with
this, I go on to his next Chapter, under
this Title,

Immorality encourag'd by the Stage.

Which Title he explains thus; *The
Stage-Poets make their principal Perfons
vicious, and reward them at the End of
their Plays.* Now here I defire to know
what his Opinion of thofe Plays would
have been, in cafe they had punifh'd thofe
vicious Perfons? Would the Punifhment
have taken off any thing from the Danger, or aton'd for the Reprefentation of
the Vice, or not? If he fays it would,
then

then that is a very fair Declaration in favour of our Stage-Diſcipline; if it would
not, then why does he pretend to blame
our Poets for not doing of that, which,
had it been done, would, in his Opinion, have ſignify'd juſt nothing at all.
Certainly Mr. *Collier* takes a more than
ordinary Delight in laſhing our Poets, o-
therwiſe he would never have thought of
making a Rod for their Stage-Diſcipline,
to carry on the Diverſion; the Smart of
which, if rightly apply'd, muſt neceſſarily light on his own Back: Tho' our
Poets deſerve it, I muſt confeſs, but not
from him; his Confidence is nothing the
leſs for their Demerits. With the ſame
Confidence he makes a mighty Noiſe,
and argues very ſtrenuouſly, under this
Head, to prove Inſtruction, and not
Pleaſure, to be the true End of Plays.
But to what purpoſe all this Flutter, all
theſe Grimaces! ſince there is a certain
Spaniard that tells us, and Mr. *Collier* is
perfectly of that *Spaniard's* Mind, as we
ſhall ſee hereafter, That let our Plays be
never ſo good, never ſo inſtructive, yet
will the Play-houſe be a Place hated by
God and haunted by the Devil, and all
that is ſaid there but Poiſon handſomly
prepar'd. Now this Mr. *Collier's* manner
of trifling with our Poets, puts me in
mind

View, *p.* 276.

mind of a Story, which tho' something old and very common, yet for the Ingenuity of it, may serve well enough to match with his pretty Tale of the Wheel-barrow. And this it is; A certain Person, a very great Lover of Cucumbers, goes to a Friend of his, who had some small Insight into Physick, but was much better skill'd in the Art of Cookery, desiring to know of him how he might so dress his Cucumbers, as to be least offensive to his Stomach. His Friend readily complying with his Desire, first, says he, pare them, then slice them into thin Slices, then squeeze them well between two Plates, then pour on them a large Quantity of the best Oil, then sprinkle them boldly with Pepper, then——but there pausing a little; And what then? says the other. Why then, replies his Friend, e'en throw them out upon the Dunghil. The Story is a *Propos*, and the Application easie, so I shall leave it to the Reader. I should now have done with Mr. *Collies* as a Reformer, but that there are still some few Strokes under this Head, tending that way, that must be consider'd.

He pretends that our Poets make too bold with Quality; they do not only ridicule our honest substantial Citizens, but even our Magistrates, our Justices of
the

Reply to Mr. Cong. Amend. p. 55.

the Peace, our Gentlemen, Efquires, Knights, nay fometimes our Lords are the Subject of their Rallery; contrary to the ancient and laudable Cuftom of their Predeceffors, who, for the moft part, contented themfelves with Coblers, Tinkers, Taylors, Dray-men, &c. Tho' therein I cannot but think they were very much out; for Humour being the Life of Comedy, and a true, eafie and natural Reprefentation of Humour the greateft Excellence of a Comick Poet; and not to be attain'd to but by a great deal of Obfervation; to what a tedious Slavery of an inferior Converfation muft our Poets be condemn'd, before they can be fuppos'd to be any thing tolerably qualify'd to attempt any thing of that kind. But that is not the only Inconvenience, for when they have done all they can, when they are never fo well qualify'd, how fhall an Audience ever judge rightly of their Performance? For that confifting, for the moft part, of Perfons of a much more elevated Condition than thofe reprefented on the Stage, and confequently unacquainted with their low Humours, can never throughly difcern that Art with which thofe Humours are touch'd and manag'd by the Poet; and yet therein confift the chiefeft Beauty of a Comedy: Nor fhall they

they meet with that Pleasure, or receive that Satisfaction they would certainly find in a due Representation of such Humours as almost every Day fall within the Compass of their Conversation. Mr. *Collier* himself seems to be of the same Opinion, when he tells us, *The Diversion* View, p. 205. *ought to be suited to the Audience, for nothing pleases which is disproportion'd to Capacity and Gust. The Rudenesses and broad Jests of Beggars, are just as acceptable to Ladies as their Rags and Cleanliness.*

But to all this it may be objected, that tho' the Poets formerly attempted none but such low Humours, yet their Plays took very well, and our Forefathers laugh'd heartily at them. And what of all that? even so do we, their wise Children, laugh as heartily at the Buffoonries of a Scaramouch, a Harlequin, or a Jack-Pudding; we are surpriz'd into a Fit of Laughter, tho' the Pleasure we take be at the same time so sickly, that it very rarely out-lives the Fit.

Whereas true Humour, well and nicely represented, gives us a more lasting, a more manly Satisfaction; it touches us to the Quick, makes a much deeper Impression on our Minds at the present, and afterwards affords Variety of Matter for

H   the

the Judgment to work upon, in order to
a convenient Regulation of our former
Extravagances. From what has been said,
I think 'tis plain that the ancient Poets
were in a great Error, whilst they confin'd themselves to such very low Characters. But whether, on the other side,
our modern Writers may not have trans-
gress'd the nicer Rules of Decency, in
attacking the Nobility, I shall not pretend to determine. Mr. *Congreve* de-
fends the Practice of our Poets in that
Particular, by that of the *French;* and
cites Mr. *Rapine* to prove that *Moliere*
frequently made bold with the Court,
in particular the Marquisses, who certainly were Courtiers, and Persons of great
Quality, if you'll believe Mr. *Rapine;*
or, if you'll rather believe Mr. *Collier,*
they were nothing less, meer Pretenders
only, and not to be reckon'd amongst
the real Nobility. Well 'tis for the Marquiss *de Louvois,* that great Minister of
State, that he's dead; for had he been
living, and had taken a Fancy to come
Reply to into *England,* according to Mr. *Collier's*
Mr. Cong. Heraldy, he must have yielded the Pass
Amend. p. to our puisne Baron. A strange and un-
27. heard of Piece of Confidence this in
Mr. *Collier!* that he, a meer Stranger,
should pretend to know the Customs of
France

France better than Mr. *Rapine,* a Native, a Man of Worth and Learning, one whom he himself often quotes with Respect, whenever he's so happy as to say any thing for his purpose; but now the Case is alter'd, and he tax'd with Misrepresenting. For thus Mr. *Collier* closes this Dispute. *But after all, if* Rapine, *plain* Rapine *now, has misreported* Moliere, *and given him more Liberty than he took, it makes nothing to Mr.* Congreve's *Purpose; for the Force of the Testimony does not lye in what* Rapine *has said, but in what* Moliere *has written.* Mr. *Rapine,* it seems, says that *Moliere* often made bold with People of Quality, and the Court. Now then let us hear *Moliere* speak for himself, and see what Mr. *Collier* will get by it. In one of his Plays he makes *Dorante,* who there certainly represents the Poet, tho' under the Title of a Chevalier, speak thus; *La Cour a quelques Ridicules, j'en demeure d'accord; & je suis, comme on voit, le premier, a les fronder.* In another Play of his he makes *Brecourt,* who, under the same Title, represents the same Poet, return this Answer to a Marquiss, that vainly pretended *Moliere* had run himself to the End of his Line, and would in a little time want Characters for the Stage;

Reply to Mr. Cong. *Amend.* p. 29.

La Critiq; de l'Escole de femmes p. 276.

L'impromptu de Versailles, p. 111.

Crois tu qu'il ait épuisé, dans ses Comedies, tout le Ridicule des Hommes? & Sons Sortier de la Cour, n'at il pas encore vingt Characteres des Gens, où il n'a pas touche? And now, where-ever the Force of the Testimony may lye, whether in Mr. *Rapine*'s Report, or in what *Moliere* himself has written, it is much at one to our Author's Purpose; since both *Rapine* and *Moliere* are against him. And that he very well knew before, since one of his Quotations on this Occasion is taken from the same Play, the same Act, the same Scene, and the very same Page, with the last of those two that I have produc'd from *Moliere*; nay there are but ten Lines between 'em. But he winks hard, I suppose, when he has no mind to see; in hopes, perhaps, that others may be as blind as he's pleas'd to make himself.

But notwithstanding what has been said, and tho', I think, it cannot be deny'd but that *Moliere* did frequently make bold with the Court, and some Persons almost of the greatest Quality in *France*; yet for my own part, I must confess, I have so great a Veneration for our Nobility, that I could wish the Example would not be follow'd here in *England*. For I cannot but think our Poets oblig'd

to

to a strict Observation of all, even the
nicest Rules of Decency, as far as may
be; that is, so long as there appears no
absolute Necessity of their breaking in upon them; which, I am confident, cannot
be pretended in this Case: Since there
ever has been, and in all probability ever
will be so great a Freedom of Conversation between our Nobility and Gentry,
that a Lord cannot possibly be infected
with any sort of Folly so peculiar to his
Quality, but that the Poet may well e-
nough suppose any Gentleman liable to
the same. And then where's the Necessity of exposing the Peer, when the Com-
moner may serve the Turn? For the Humour, on the Stage, becoming the one
every whit as well as the other, must
needs be equally instructive and divert-
ing to both. And so I have done with
this Head.

I should now go on to his Fifth Chapter; but that consisting altogether of some
Remarks on three particular Plays, some
to his Purpose, some not, but all beside
mine, I shall here take my Leave of
Mr. *Collier* as a Reformer, and proceed to
his Sixth Chapter, where I shall be oblig'd to consider him as an Enemy. For
there making a very notable Collection
of all he could meet with, any way re-

H 3   flecting

flecting either on Plays or Players, he
pretends to shew

The Opinion of the Pagans, of the Church, and State, concerning the Stage.

Under this Head then, our Author
pretends to give his Reader a short View
of the Sense of Antiquity, back'd by
some Modern Authorities, concerning
the Stage: *From all which,* he says, *it
will appear that Plays have been generally look'd upon as the Nurseries of Vice,
the Corrupters of Youth, and the Grievance
of the Country where they are suffer'd.*
Very good: And now, I suppose, no
body will blame me for treating Mr. *Collier* as an Enemy, after such a hearty Declaration as this. Here's no Distinction
of Plays, good or bad, they all fall under the same Censure. But to proceed:
Mr. *Collier* ranges his Proof from Testimony, as he calls it, under these three
Heads.

View, *p.*
233.

Under the First he cites some Heathen
Philosophers, Historians, Orators, and
Poets.

The

The Second confifts of the Laws and Conftitutions of Princes, and the Authentick Reports of infallible Gazettes.

The Third is drawn from Church Records, from Fathers, and Councils of unexceptionable Authority.

I begin with his Pagan Authors. *All Men,* as he tells us, *of the biggeft Confideration for Senfe, Learning, and Figure.* And pretty big indeed they had need be, that muft be thought to comprehend the Senfe of Antiquity on this Subject. But let 'em be as big as they will, I doubt not but I fhall match 'em prefently, nay and perhaps overmatch 'em too. Here then I defire to know whether Plays were not publickly reprefented, in thofe feveral Nations or Countries where thofe Heathen Authors liv'd, which he has now mufter'd up againft them? But of that, I think, there need be no Queftion made; for why elfe did they complain? Now Plays cannot be fuppos'd to be acted any where, but with the Allowance of the higher Powers: Nor can that Allowance amount to any thing lefs than an Approbation; for no body certainly will allow the free Exercife of any thing they do not approve of. And if fo, then you have here, at one View, thoufands rifing up in Defence

Ibid.

H 4   of

of the Stage, againft every one of his Gigantick Pagans; that is, you have the Senfe of the governing Part, (which I think I may modeftly enough affirm to be ever the wifeft) not only of thofe very Nations where they writ, but of all other Kingdoms or Countries where Plays have been at any time allow'd, from their firft Original to this Day. Not to infift upon many thoufands of illuftrious Perfons befide, who have at all times gladly frequented them; which furely they would never have done, had they look'd on them as Nurferies only of Vice, and Corrupters of Youth. This now I think a much fairer Account of the Senfe of Antiquity concerning Plays, than what our Author has offer'd from the Teftimony of eight or ten Perfons only, of what Fame or Learning foever they may otherwife have been. But after all, of what Nature is this Heathen Teftimony he makes fuch a mighty Noife about? What do thofe Gentlemen Pagans fay againft the Stage, that can make good the heavy Charge Mr. *Collier* has given in againft all Plays in general? Let us fee that a little.

He begins with *Plato*, who tells us that Plays raife the Paffions, and pervert the Ufe of them, and by confequence are dangerous to Morality; for this Reafon

he

he banishes Poets (not Plays in particu- View, *p. 5.*
lar). his Common-wealth. So indeed
says our Author: But Sir *Philip Sidney,*
a Gentleman pretty well acquainted with
Plato, is quite of another Opinion. " A *Defence of*
" Man might ask, says he, out of what *Poetry.*
" Common-wealth *Plato* doth banish Po-
" ets? In sooth thence, where he himself
" alloweth Community of Women. So
" as belike this Banishment grew not for
" effeminate. Wantonness; since little
" should Poetical Sonnets be hurtful,
" when a Man might have what Woman
" he listed. St. *Paul* himself sets a watch
" Word upon Philosophy, indeed upon
" the Abuse: So doth *Plato* upon the A-
" buse, not upon Poetry. *Plato* found
" fault that the Poets of his Time fill'd
" the World with wrong Opinions of the
" Gods: Tho' the Poets did not induce
" such Opinions, but did imitate such O-
" pinions already induc'd. Who list may
" read in *Plutarch* the Discourses of *Isis*
" and *Osiris,* of the Cause why Oracles
" ceas'd, of the Divine Providence, and
" see whether the Theology of that Na-
" tion stood not upon such Dreams, which
" the Poets indeed supersticiously obser-
" ved. And truly, since they had not
" the Light of Christ, did much better
" in it than the Philosophers; who shak-
" ing

" ing off Superstition, brought in A-
" theism. But a Man need go no farther
" than to *Plato* himself, to know his
" Meaning; who in his Dialogue call'd
" *Ion*, giveth high and rightly Divine
" Commendations unto Poetry. For in-
" deed, I had rather, since truly I may
" do it, shew their mistaking of *Plato*,
" who, under his Lion's Skin, makes an
" Ass-like Braying against Poesie, than
" go about to overthrow his Authority;
" whom, the wiser a Man is, the more
" just Cause he shall find to have in Ad-
" miration. Especially since he attribu-
" teth unto Poesie more than my self do,
" namely, to be a very Inspiring, of Di-
" vine Force, far above Man's Wit; as
" in the afore-nam'd Dialogue is appa-
" rent.

Xenophon, a great Philosopher, and famous Captain, appears next; and he
commends the *Persian* Discipline: *They
won't*, says he, *so much as suffer their
Youth to hear any thing that is amorous
or tawdry.* But may there not be Plays,
wherein there may be nothing either a-
morous or tawdry? Yes certainly, and
most of *Corneille*'s Tragedies are notable
Instances of that Truth. And what then
has *Xenophon* to say against them?

Mr. Col-

Mr. *Collier,* I perceive, is hard put to it, and ready to catch at every Twig; otherwise honest *Aristotle,* who took so much Pains to reduce Poetry into an Art, had never been lugg'd in by the Ears, to give his Testimony against Plays. But he, when he says he would have young People forbid by the Law the seeing of Players; as also when he speaks of the Force of Musick and Action, in commanding and changing the Passions, as things of a dangerous Consequence in Plays; he, I say, in both those Cases, must be understood of loose, irregular and lascivious Pieces. For beside that *Show, Musick, Action and Rhetorick are moving Entertainments, and, rightly employ'd, would be very significant;* that great Philosopher, had he meant any thing more, must needs have given himself as severe a Rebuff, as he could be thought to give the Stage.

Introd. to his View, p. 1.

Next comes the *Roman* Orator *Tully;* but he cries out only upon licentious Plays and Poems, as the Bane of Sobriety and wise Thinking. And who ever was of any other Opinion? But he says likewise, that Comedy subsists upon Lewdness; and that, I say, is evidently false, there being many Plays extant that have nothing lewd in them. He objects
farther,

Tacitus comes next, who relating how *Nero* hir'd decay'd Gentlemen for the Stage, complains of his Mismanagement, in driving them to an ill Practice, rather than relieving their Necessities. And certainly *Nero* did very ill in tempting Gentlemen to a Profession so much below them. But what of that? Because Gentlemen should not be made Players, must Plays therefore needs be the Nurseries of Vice, and the Corrupters of Youth? But he says likewise, that the *German* Women were guarded against Danger, and kept their Honour out of harm's way, by having no Play-Houses among them. Now this I take to be a severer Reflection on the *German* Women than on Plays, and Mr. *Collier*, methinks, makes pretty bold with our modern Ladies, when he quotes *Tacitus* to so lewd a Purpose. For what may be said of them, if loss of Honour, to speak no plainer, must be look'd on as a necessary Consequence of their frequenting the Play-house. But if ever any such thing happen'd, the Loss, I am apt to believe, was not very great, and that they brought but very little Honour with them to lose, that lost it there.

Plutarch says no more than that Plays are dangerous to corrupt young People, and is to be understood only of loose, ir-

regular

regular Pieces: For so our Author himself understands him, as plainly appears
from the Inference he draws from his
Words; *And therefore,* says he, *Stage-
Poetry, when it grows too hardy, ought to
be check'd*; and I am perfectly of the same
Mind, if that be all he pretends to. But
then how strangely flat is he fall'n, and
what would he have to say against Plays,
supposing our Stage-Poetry not too hardy? As such a thing may well be, whatever is or has been.

And now I have done with his Heathen Philosophers, Orators and Historians, he closes all with a Brace of Pagan
Poets, *Ovid* and Mr. *Wycherly*; the last,
no doubt on't, is mightily oblig'd to him
for giving him a Place among his Heathen Worthies: But let that pass.

Ovid, in his Book *De Arte Amandi,*
tells his Reader, That nothing was more
common than to see Beauty surpriz'd,
Women debauch'd, and Wenches pick'd
up at these Diversions, meaning Plays.
But what of all that? What if *Ovid* did
recommend the Play-house to some such
lewd Sparks as himself, as a Place likely
to afford Game enough; is it such a wonderful thing, that amongst a great many
Women of Virtue and Honour, some
Whores should crowd in? And are not
all

all great and publick Affemblies liable to
the fame Inconvenience? When *Ovid* in
his Remedy of Love, forbids the feeing of
Plays and reading of Poets, he is to be un-
derftood of Irregular Plays and fuch lafci-
vious Poems as many of his own were ;
and for which he there pretends to cry *Pec-
cavi.* In his *De Triftibus* indeed, he advifes
Auguftus to fupprefs the Stage : But did
Auguftus take his Advice? No certainly ;
that great Monarch look'd on it as impertinent then; and therefore, as fuch, I
think we may very well pafs it by now.

Mr. *Wycherly* brings up the Rear of all
his Pagan Authorities, and he has plac'd
him there, I fuppofe, as in a Poft of Honour, for the notable Service he has done
the Party. He, fays our Author, in his
Dedication to Lady *B.* an eminent Pro-
curefs, pleads the Merits of his Funtion,
and infifts on being Billeted upon free
Quarter, for convening the Cullies at the
Theatres to be pick'd up and carried to
a Supper, and Bed at her Houfe. *This,*
fays our Author, is frank Evidence, and
ne'er the lefs true for the Air of a Jeft.
And yet let it be as true as it will, it
makes nothing at all againft Plays, as I
have already fhewn. For, if Wenches
and their Cullies, under the Pretence of
feeing a Play, will take that Opportunity
of

View, *p.*
240.

of jugging together .in the Play-houfe, who can help it? This poffibly might be a good Argument for the putting down all publick, promifcuous Affemblies, were the Thing feafible; but it can never be reafonably urg'd againft Plays in particular, unlefs our Author will pretend to prove, that there are no Fools or Whores to be met with any where but in a Playhoufe. But alas! no Places are free from fuch Vermin, even our Churches have been profan'd by their Intrigues, and Wenches there pick'd up; and yet it never enter'd into the Head of any one, that ever I heard of, to cenfure either the Preachers or their Sermons on that account. But our Author may object yet farther, that Mr. *Wycherly* here brags of his Service, and claims a Reward of the Bawd, as if he wrote for no other purpofe but to draw in Cullies to quicken their Practice; if he did fo, fo much the worfe for him, he muft anfwer for it. The Fault is perfonal, and cannot affect our Plays, nor thofe other Poets that write with a nobler Defign than he has endeavour'd to make the World believe he did; tho' for my own part, I muft confefs I cannot eafily entertain fo very mean an Opinion of fo ingenious a Gentleman as Mr. *Wycherly.*

I   And

And, now we have heard all his Heathen Witnesses, what do they prove? How poorly do they maintain that mighty Huff of his, against all Plays, in the Beginning of this Chapter; for I dare boldly affirm, that there's not any one of them that comes up to the Purpose for which he was Cited: And so I leave them, and proceed to his Censures of State, where he pretends to shew how much the Stage stands discourag'd by the Laws of other Countries and by our own. Thus, the farther he drives on his Design against Plays, the worse, for ought as I can find, he likes it, at least he dwindles strangely in his Pretensions; for whereas before he could talk of nothing less than the Banishment of the Poets, the Suppression of Plays, or the utter Overthrow of the Play-houses, he is now contented to fly at small Game, rather than not to be doing; and to shew us how far Plays have been discourag'd only. And yet I doubt he will go near to fall short of his Aim there too; for certainly the State might, at any time, as easily have put down Plays as discourag'd them. However let's see wherein lyes this great Discouragement he talks of. In the first place, he

tells us, *That the* Athenians, *none of the*

worst

worst Friends to the Play-house, made a Law that no Judge of the Areopagus *should write Plays.* And what of that? Because they did not think it fit, that their Judges should neglect the weightier Affairs of State, only to amuse themselves with writing of Plays, must Comedy therefore be look'd upon as so unreputable a Performance? Wit is the only thing I know of, in this World, to which all Mankind in general make some Pretensions; nor is there any Prize so passionately desir'd, or pursu'd with so much eager Emulation, as that of Wit. No wonder then if the *Athenians,* wisely apprehending the dangerous Consequences of so violent an Emulation amongst their Magistrates, should by a Law forbid them all such publick Trials of Skill. And this now I take to be a more probable Account of the Reason of that Law, than that our Author pretends to give us, since there's nothing more certain, than that no People ever encourag'd Wit and Poetry, Plays and Players, more than the *Athenians.* But the *Lacedemonians,* he says, *would not endure the Stage in any Form, nor under any Regulation;* but what signifies the Example of a handful of Men against the Practice of all *Greece,*

Ibid.

I 2   nay

nay of all the civiliz'd World? However, waving that, it may be said, that perhaps the *Lacedemonians* knew little, or, rather nothing at all of Plays, and therefore cannot properly be said, either to condemn or discourage what they did not understand. But supposing that upon mature Deliberation they rejected Plays, so did they likewise all other Diversions whatsoever that were not altogether Martial. In short, they were a People wholly addicted to War, and tho' we cannot allow Plays to be the Nurseries of Vice, yet never any body, that I know of, pretended to cry them up as the most proper Nurseries of War; tho', when all is done, I believe it may be easily enough made appear, that *Athens,* that glorious Seat of the Muses, bred as many brave Captains as ever the *Lacedemonians* with their rough and almost savage Education could boast of. *Tully,* says our Author, *informs us that their Predecessors accounted all Stage-Plays uncreditable and scandalous.* He should have told us by what Act of State they had been declar'd such, otherwise his Testimony, under this Head at least, is but Impertinent. Besides, his saying that Plays were in former times look'd on as Scandalous, is, as I take it, a plain Confession, that they were not thought fo in his; and a very probable Argument, that there were no fuch Laws then at leaft in force, either againft Plays or Players as he talks of. Not to infift, as a farther Confirmation of the fame Opinion, on his own great Familiarity with *Rofcius* and *Æfop,* two admirable Actors in thofe Times. But what if Players were held Infamous, muft Plays therefore needs be Scandalous? That would be but an odd kind of an Inference; for at that rate of arguing, Juftice it felf muft fall into Difgrace, fince all her fevereft Decrees are executed by an infamous Hand: And yet on this rotten Foundation it is, that he pretends to raife this terrible Battery, againft the Reputation of Plays. For having little, or rather nothing to fay against them under this Head, he vents all his Malice, and lets fly all his Artillery againft Players; tho' unlefs he can prove that they were held Infamous, meerly on the Account of their acting of Plays, he only beats the Air, but proves nothing. It is very certain that Players, however they may have been Cenfur'd by fome People and in fome Countries, have been as much favour'd and cherifh'd in others; and *Greece* was every whit as kind as *Rome* could be fevere to them; tho', by the by, 'tis a moot Point amongft the Doctors, whe-

whether, by the *Roman* Laws, Players are infamous or no. Now, tho' our Plays, and our Players too, are to ftand or fall by our own Laws, and not thofe of any other Country whatfoever; yet be-caufe Mr. *Collier* is pleas'd to infift fo much on his *Roman* Authorities, let us fee how far they will go towards the prov-ing Players infamous, even by the Ci-vil Law.

View. p. 241.

We read in Livy, *fays our Author, that the young People in* Rome *kept the* Fabulæ Atellanæ *to themfelves, they would not fuffer that Diverfion to be ble-mifh'd by the Stage: And for that Reafon, the Actors of the* Fabulæ Atellanæ *were nei-ther expell'd their Tribe, nor refus'd to ferve in Arms. Both which Penalties it appears the common Players lay under.* Well; and what now does our Author pretend to prove from all this? Were not the *Fabulæ Atellanæ* Plays? And were not thofe *Roman* Youngfters that acted them, Players? Both *Livy* and he call them fo in exprefs Terms: Nay cer-tainly they were fo, and if that be grant-ed, as I think it cannot be deny'd, then we have here, Thanks to our Author, a full and undeniable Inftance of Plays, that were not thought fcandalous; and of Players too, that were not cenfur'd as

in-

infamous. So unlucky is our Author in
his Proofs from Teſtimony, that he ſeldom pretends to any thing of Authority,
but that it makes as much or more indeed againſt than for him. Thus we
have here already gain'd this one conſiderable Point, by his Quotation from *Livy*,
that Players were not eſteem'd Infamous,
or puniſh'd either on the Account of their
Profeſſion, or of the Plays they acted; as
will appear yet plainer, if we conſider
the Nature of thoſe *Fabulæ Atellanæ* he
ſo much boaſts of, and that were not, as
he ſays, to be prophan'd by the Common
Players. From what *Livy* ſays of them,
we may conclude that they were Ridiculous, or Comical. *Juventus*, ſays he,
*Hiſtrionibus fabularum actu relicto, ip-
ſa inter ſe more antiquo, ridicula intexta
verſibus jactitare cæpit: quæ inde Exodia
poſtea apellata, conſertaque fabellis po-
tiſſimum Atellanis ſunt. Godelevæus*, in
his Annotations on that Author, gives
this farther Account of them. *Atellanæ autem*, ſays he, *non totæ, Sedearum
Actus aliquis Tragediis interponebantur,
e Scena digreſſis Tragedis: Ita, quod ex-
tra Tragediæ argumentum digreſſis Tragedis agerentur, Exodia vocabantur. Ut
enim Satiræ, Græcis Tragediis interponebantur, Tragediis Latinis, ad exhiliran-*
dum

dum Spectatorem, Atellanarum Exodia interserebantur. *Juvenal* likewise repreſents thoſe *Exodia* as meerly Comical.

Lib. 2.
Satyr. 6.

> *Urbicus Exodio riſum movet Atellanæ*
> *Geſtibus Autœnes* ——

And the learned *Lubin,* in his Comment on this Paſſage in that Poet, agrees perfectly with *Godelevæus* in his Account of theſe *Exodia;* only he ſpeaks ſomething broader. *Erat hoc,* ſays he, *in Atellanis Fabulis Exodium, ridiculum & obſcenum Carmen, quod Tragedis egreſſis, apud Latinos ſolebat ab Exodiariis recitari, ad exhilarandos Spectatores,* &c. And a little lower he ſpeaks thus, *Erant autem Fabulæ Atellanæ propriæ, quæ res Serias, in riſim convertebant,* &c. And *Stephanus,* under the Word *Atella,* takes notice of them and ſays, they were *Comediæ joculares & ſcarriles.*

And now, I think, 'tis plain enough, that theſe *Fabulæ Atellanæ* were no better than Farces, and thoſe too Satyrical and Obſcene, Lewd and Scurrilous; and therefore, I think, we may reaſonably enough conclude, that tho' the common Players were ſo cenſur'd, as *Livy* ſeems to intimate, yet was it not meerly on the Account of their Calling, nor of the

Play they acted; since 'tis very plain,
that the *Romans*, at the same time, allow'd of and incourag'd other Players,
and no Plays could well be more scandalous than those *Fabulæ Atellanæ* were.

In the Theodosian *Code*, *Players are*   Ibid.
call'd, Personæ inhonestæ, *and that is*,
says our Author, *to translate it softly*,
Persons maim'd and blemish'd in their Re-
putation. Very soft indeed! and the
Players, no doubt on't, are infinitely
oblig'd to him for his great Civility.
But what if we should find out yet a
softer Translation, and that too counte-
nanced by the Law? It is no very un-
likely thing to be done, I'll assure you,
nor indeed do I at all despair of it: Since,
according to our Author's usual Address
in these Matters, he himself is so happy
as to point to the very Place, where we
cannot miss of it. For whilst he tells us,
that to the utter Disgrace and Confusion
of all Players, their Pictures were not
any longer allow'd to hang cheek by joll
with the Emperors, we find the Words
of the Law, in that Case, to run thus.
Neque unquam post hac liceat, in loco ho-   Cod. de.
nesto, in honestas adnotare, personas. And   Spect. L.
Gothofred notes on the Text, thus, *Inho-*   si qua, 4.
nestas Personas, non esse pro infamibus
accipiendas existimant, sed pro abjectis,
&

& vilibus, quæ inter honeſtas numerari non debent. Now tho' the Word *exiſtimant* may ſeem to repreſent this, as the Opinion of others, rather than his own; yet I cannot think it ever the leſs authentick for that. For beſide that he himſelf owns it as a general Opinion taken up, without any the leaſt Offer of proving it falſe or erroneous, he likewiſe gives us the Reaſon on which that Opinion was grounded. *Ne pugnet,* ſays he, *lex Athletas, cum hac lege.* And indeed I cannot ſee how theſe two Laws can be any otherwiſe reconcil'd, than by the Admiſſion of that favourable Interpretation of theſe Words, *Perſonæ inhoneſtæ*: Thus all the Softneſs of Mr. *Collier*'s Tranſlation is vaniſh'd in an Inſtant, and no Wonder at all; for Softneſs is by no means his Talent. Well; but Players, ſays our Author, are *Famoſi ex Edicto,* and I grant it. But than we muſt conſider, that the Prætors Edicts, by which they were ſo cenſur'd, were, as arbitrary, ſo but temporary; they were but the Diceſions of particular Men, and no longer in Force than thoſe particular Men were in Power; that is, one Year. Unleſs perhaps they were taken up and impos'd a-new by ſome ſucceeding Prætors, or by the Emperors afterwards added to their Laws; which yet

F. de his qui not. infam. L. 4.

yet seldom hapned, without some Altera-
tion, or Limitation of them. Thus, in
the Case before us, we have the Prætors
Edict in these general Words: *Infamia*
notatur, qui Artis ludicræ, pronuncian-
dive causa, in Scenam prodierit. But
when this Edict came afterwards to be
incorporated into the Law, it was plainly limited, by an explanatory Addition.
For thus says *Ulpian, Eos, qui quæstus*
causa in certamina descendunt, & omnes,
propter præmium, in Scenam prodeuntes,
famosos esse Pegassus, & nerva filius re-
sponderunt. *Gothofred* here indeed cries
out, *Imo & qui sine quæstu, Omnes enim*
Scinici probosi. But then 'tis to be observ'd, that he offers no Law to confirm
that his Opinion; but quotes St. *Au-*
gustine, and *Livy,* two very extraordinary Men indeed but no Lawyers; and consequently of no very great Authority in
Matters meerly of Law. And now it
appears plainly enough, I think, that
Players, even by the *Roman* Laws, are
not accounted Infamous, meerly for
acting of Plays; for unless they do it,
quæstus causa, they stand clear. So that
we have here, at last, why Players by
that Law have been held Infamous; and
that was, only because they were Merce-
nary. But alas! does not that Reason
strike

F. de his
not. inf.
L. Præt. 1.

strike equally at all Professions whatsoever? Yes certainly; for at that rate the Lawyer shall be condemn'd that pleads, and the Physician that prescribes for his Fee; nor shall we little Authors escape, that write Books and sell the Copies.

And now we are come to our own Constitutions, where I find, says our Author, by the 39 *Eliz.* Cap. 4. that all Bearwards, common Players of Enterludes, counterfeit *Egyptians,* &c. shall be taken, adjudg'd, and deem'd Rogues, Vagabonds, and sturdy Beggars; and shall sustain all Pain and Punishment, as by this Act is, in that behalf, appointed. A very fair Quotation this indeed! and, as he has order'd Matters, very pat to his Purpose. But certainly Mr. *Collier* thinks himself Privileg'd to say or do any thing. He is not contented with misrepresenting a Parcel of old Philosophers, Orators, and Poets, but he must be tampering too with our Laws; which he maims and mangles at his Pleasure, 'till he can rack them to his own Sense. Thus he leaves out two very material Words, two Words so absolutely necessary to the right Understanding of the Law, and so many several times repeated, in that very Paragraph from whence his Quotation

is

is taken, that I am in amaze how he durſt venture to ſuppreſs them, I dare boldly affirm that Law to be not only cruel and unjuſt, but ridiculous and nonſenſical. For, according to that his Manner of repreſenting it, not only Players, but all Scholars, Proctors, and Sea-faring Men, are liable to the Penal-ties there impos'd on Rogues, Vaga-bonds, and ſturdy Beggars, and that too, whether they beg, ſteal, or ramble about the Country, or not. Whereas that Law was made only to ſuppreſs all Stroulers, or Idle Perſons, wandring a-bout the Country, and under plauſible Pretences comitting ſeveral Diſorders, as appears by the Title. In order to which excellent End, it tells us who ſhall be adjudg'd, deem'd and reputed as ſuch; a very neceſſary Caution, where the Pe-nalty was to be ſo ſevere. The Words of the Act then run thus. All Perſons calling themſelves Scholars, *Going about beg-ging:* All Sea-faring Men, pretending Loſs of Goods, or Ship, *Going about the Country begging:* All Idle Perſons, *go-ing about in any Country,* either *begging,* or uſing any *ſubtle Craft,* &c. All Pro-ctors, Procurers, Patent-Gatherers, or Collectors for Goals, Priſons, or Hoſpi-tals, all Fencers, Bearwards, common Play-

Players of Enterludes, and Minstrels, *Wandring abroad,* &c. *All wandring* Persons, and common Labourers, refusing to work, *&c.* All Juglers, Tinkers, Pedlars, and Petty Chapmen, *Wandring abroad:* All Persons deliver'd out of Goals that *beg* for their Fees, or otherwise do *Travel begging:* All such Persons that shall *Wander abroad begging,* pretending Loss by Fire, or otherwise: And all such Persons, not being Fellons, *Wandering* and pretending themselves to be *Ægyptians,* or *Wandring* in the Habit, Form or Attire of counterfeit *Ægyptians;* shall be taken, adjudg'd and deem'd Rogues, Vagabonds and sturdy Beggars, *&c.* I have been the more particular in transcribing the greatest Part of this Paragraph, that the Reader may the better perceive the great Care our Lawmakers took in the Penning of this Act, to prevent all manner of Mistakes, whether ignorant or malicious, by the frequent Repetition of those very significant Words, which Mr. *Collier* has thought fit to cut off with an *& cætera,* as impertinent, because not for his Purpose: But notwithstanding all his little Shifts, I think 'tis very plain, that 'tis not in reality either the Scholar, the Proctor, the Sea-faring Man, or the Player, that

is

is cenfur'd by this Law; but the Strou-
ler, the Rogue, the Vagabond, and the
fturdy Beggar. In fhort, this Act touches not thofe Players that are Licens'd by
any Peer of the Land; much lefs thofe
that are Authoris'd by the King's (or
Queen's) Patent, or honour'd with the
Title of his (or her Majefty's) Servants.
Well: But our Author tells us, that by
another later Act, *viz.* 1. *Jac.* I. Cap.
7. the Privilege of Licenfing is taken
away; and all of them, meaning the
Players, exprefly brought under the Penalty without Diftinction. Over Shoes,
over Boots, as the good old Proverb has
it. Mr. *Collier*'s Hand is in, and he knows
not when to give over his pretty Tricks.
For here now he quotes an Act of
Parliament that is expir'd, and has been
out of Doors above thefe threefcore Years.
But fuppofing it ftill in Force, and that
it did Curtal the Privilege of the Peers,
in the Matter of Licenfing of Players,
yet I cannot think it touch'd the King's
Prerogative in that Particular, and then
they are fafe enough. But I don't love to
talk without Book, I muft confefs I cannot yet get a Sight of that Statute at large,
and therefore I fhall fay no more of it,
but leave our Author to make what Advantage he can of his no Law.

About

About the Year 1580, fays our Author, there was a Petition made to Queen
Elizabeth, for the fuppreffing of Play-
houfes; 'tis fomewhat remarkable, fays
he, and therefore I fhall tranfcribe fome
Part of the Relation. *Many Godly Citizens.* Hold, Sir, hold, we have enough
on't; and I am confident there can be
nothing more remarkable in it, than the In-
folence of that their Pharifaical Beginning.
By thofe few Words therefore, I doubt
not but the Reader will eafily guefs
what fort of People thofe Godly Petitioners were: A fort of People, then firft
beginning to peep abroad, under the
plaufible Mask of an extraordinary Piety;
whofe chief Devotion however confifted
in Contradiction : A fort of People, who
under the Pretence of Religion, and a
tender Confcience, were even then form-
ing a dangerous Faction againft the State;
and therefore thought fit to ftile themfelves the Godly, that they might the
better carry on their ungodly Practices :
A fort of People, that would cheat with
an Ejaculation in their Mouths, and at
any time rather tell a hundred Lies, than
hear one Oath: A Sort of People, in fhort, as
liket hofe Pharifees of old, againft whom
our Bleffed Saviour himfelf denounc'd
fo many dreadful Woes, as one Drop of
Water

Water is like another. The Perfons pe-
titioning thus known, no body fure can
doubt of their Bufinefs; and a Petition
from the Godly, handed down to Pofterity by Mr. *Collier,* muft needs be againft
thofe prophane things call'd Plays. But
pray what was the Succefs of that Petition? How was it receiv'd by the Queen,
was fhe convinc'd either of the Illegality
or Inexpediency of Plays, by that their
pious and remarkable Remonftrance?
Not at all: For Plays were not only allow'd, but encourag'd by her through the
whole Courfe of her long and glorious
Reign. The incomparable *Shakefpear*
wrote then for the Stage, and very frequently by her particular Command. But
were not the Play-houfes in the City pul-
led down then, on that Occafion? It
may be fo, for any thing I know, but
what of all that? Is it fuch a Wonder,
that a wife, good and gracious Queen
fhould leave the Government of the City
to the pious Lord Mayor, and his fancti-
fy'd Brethren; efpecially they not being
then fo well known as they have been
fince. Even that glorious Queen, wife,
as fhe was, almoft to a Miracle, could not
then fee through the dangerous Confequences of fuch an Indulgence; yet that,
and fome other Royal Condefcenfions of

K   the

the like nature, quickly gave those Petitioners an extraordinary Reputation of Sanctity, amongst the unsanctify'd Rabble, and embolden'd them afterwards, first to dispute with King *James*, and then to fight with King *Charles*; and that, if we consider them only, almost with equal Success. For it is certain, they were most notoriously baffled at *Hampton-Court*; and tho' that good, but unfortunate Prince, King *Charles* the First, sunk under the brutish Fury of their Arms, yet were they, in the height of their Hopes, outwitted, scorn'd, and piss'd upon, by a new, upstart, Mushroom Sect, sprung from their own filthy Dunghill. And so much for those godly Petitioners, and their remarkable Petition; which can signifie nothing to the Discouragement of Plays, unless perhaps Mr. *Collier*, looking on Queen *Elizabeth* as a kind of a Reprobate, may be pleas'd to think Plays, and Players, more disgrac'd in being thrust out of the City by the Godly, than honour'd in being often receiv'd and admitted, with Approbation and Encouragement, by that glorious Queen, within the Verge of her Court.

And now Room for the Gazetteer; who in the Year 1696 tells us, that the Lord Arch-Bishop of *Paris*, supported

by

by the Intereſt of ſome religious Perſons at Court, has done his utmoſt to ſuppreſs the Publick Theatres by degrees, or at leaſt to clear 'em from Prophaneſs. What! whether they were prophane or no? But to let that paſs. Did the Lord Arch-Biſhop make the Gazetteer his Confident in the Caſe? I am apt to believe not. How then came he to be ſo very well acquainted with that Prelate's Deſigns, which never had their Effect? Indeed the *French* Stage, to our Shame be it ſpoken, is, and at all times has been ſo very modeſt and reſerv'd, in all thoſe things that might give the leaſt Offence, that we might very well queſtion the Truth of ſuch a Piece of News as this, tho' coming from a more Authentick Hand, than that of a common Gazetteer. But ſuppoſe it true, and that Monſieur *l'Archivêque*, having a more than ordinary Itching after a red Hat, might hope, by appearing againſt Plays, to give the World ſuch a Sample of his Zeal for Religion, as might make ſome Noiſe at *Rome*; what is all that to the Purpoſe in hand? As for his other Piece of *Dutch* News from *France*, it may perhaps be true as to the Matter of Fact; that is, the King, it may be, did order the *Italian* Players to leave the Kingdom: But

K 2 that

that he did it for the acting of immodeft
Pieces, in Contempt of his expreſs Order to the contrary, I cannot believe. For
beſide that there is no ſmall Danger of
diſobeying his Commands, 'tis well known
that ever ſince the firſt Eſtabliſhment of
the *Italian* Players at *Paris*, the Company of *French* Actors there have made
Uſe of all their Intereſt, in ſeveral Perſons of the firſt Rank about the King,
to remove, and ſend them home again:
So that 'tis no great Wonder, if they
have at laſt prevail'd.   And that this is
the true Reaſon of the other's Diſgrace,
is more than probable, from the next
Piece of News our Author tells us. *The*
ſame Intelligence, ſays he, *the next Week*
after acquaints us, that ſome Perſons of
the greateſt Quality at Court, the Pro-
tectors of thoſe Comedians, had ſollicited
the French *King to recall his Order a-*
gainſt them: But their Requeſt had no
Succeſs. Now, I think, 'tis very unlike-
ly that any Perſons of Virtue, Honour,
and Quality, ſhould dare to intercede for
Players cenſur'd by the King himſelf, for
their Lewdneſs, Obſcenity and Diſobe-
dience: Whereas there is nothing more
probable, than that ſuch Perſons might
endeavour to ſupport the *Italian* againſt
the *French* Players, and yet miſcarry in
it too.   Having

Having done with his News Papers, our Author in the next place presents us with a sort of Pastoral Letter, publish'd by the Bishop of *Arras* in *Flanders:* But because this Letter, for the most part, contains little else but a rambling kind of a Flourish at large against Plays, grounded on the pretended Opinions of some of the Fathers and Councils, into which I shall have an Occasion to enquire farther hereafter, and ends at last in a severe Order against Players, which I must once more say is nothing at all to his Purpose against Plays; I shall here take no farther Notice of it, but for once confront this his *French* Bishop with a Cardinal of the same Nation, equally eminent in Church and State, I mean Cardinal *Richelieu;* who was so great a Lover of Wit and Poetry, in particular of Dramatick Poetry, and had so very favourable an Opinion of the Innocence and Lawfulness of that Diversion, that he himself, as 'twas thought, writ some Plays, which were acted with great Applause. As a Proof of which, the *French* tell you, that when Mr. *Corneille*'s *Cid* first appear'd on the Stage, that great Man was so sensibly touch'd at the extraordinary Applause with which that Piece was receiv'd by the World, that he

K 3

pre-

presently set all the greatest Wits of *France* to work, to enquire into the Dramatick Merits of it, indeed to censure it. And that, say they, was the Beginning of the famous Academy, which then first founded by him on that Occasion, has ever since flourish'd under the particular Protection of their King. Now tho', I must confess, that I have all this from Tradition only, yet the famous *Boileau*, in one of his excellent Satyrs, seems to confirm the Truth of it, and to justifie the Tradition almost in every Circumstance.

Satire 9. p. 81.
En vain contre le Cid, un Ministre se ligue,
Tout Paris *pour Chimene a les yeux de*
[*Roderigue:*
L'Academie en Corps, a beau le Censurer,
Le Public revolté, s'obstine a l'admirer.

Our Author, now at last, pretends to give us the Opinion of the Primitive Church concerning the Stage, and he begins with several of her Councils. Of all which however, there is but one that so much as mentions Plays; and that is the Third Council of *Carthage*, where 'tis ordain'd that the Sons of Bishops, or other Clergymen, should not be permitted to furnish out publick Shews or Plays, or
be

be prefent at them, fuch fort of Pagan
Entertainments being forbidden all the
Laity; it being always unlawful for all
Chriftians to come amongft Blafphemers.
What then! Is Blafphemy an effential
Part of Dramatick Poetry? And is it not
poffible for us to peep into a Play-houfe,
but we muft be faid prefently to herd
with Blafphemers? Certainly Mr. *Collier*
will not pretend to run things to fuch a
heighth, and if he does not, what then
does this Council fignifie againft Plays?
For my part I think it rather makes for
them, for if by this Council they ftand
condemn'd only as they are blafphemous,
remove but that Objection, which may
eafily be done, and they ftand right e-
nough, for any thing that has to fay againft
them. And indeed, I muft here tell
Mr. *Collier,* once for all, that 'till he can
produce fome one or more Councils,
wherein Plays, as Plays, tho' otherwife
never fo innocent, are plainly and in exprefs Terms condemn'd as utterly unlawful; and not only the Players for acting,
but all other People are cenfur'd for frequenting them; all his Learning, all his
Wit, all his little Arts, will fignifie juft
nothing, and he will never be able to fay
any thing much to the purpofe againft
Plays in general, however he may divert

him-

himself, with flourishing against some few particular Abuses. For what a poor Shift is he here put to, where, of seven Councils by him quoted, six are nothing at all to his purpose, as levell'd all against Players, not Plays, that is, against the Calling, the Profession, not the thing it self. For, as the Reverend and Learned Bishop *Sanderson* very judiciously observes, there may be some things lawful to do, which are not lawful to live by; some things lawful as Delights, which are not lawful as Callings. In answer therefore to our Author's Councils, which are so severe upon Players, I shall here only give him the Opinion of that learned, good and pious Prelate, concerning the Calling or Profession of a Player; who as he does not pretend to recommend it as eligible, so neither does he absolutely condemn it as sinful. He therefore lays down Three Things to be enquir'd into, before any one undertakes any thing as a Calling. *First*, Whether the thing be simply and in it self lawful or not? *Secondly*, Whether it be lawful, so as to be made a Calling or no? And, *Thirdly*, Whether it will be profitable, or rather hurtful to the Common-wealth? These Three Things premis'd, as necessary to the Election of a right Calling; he, speaking to the Second,

cond, delivers himſelf thus in the Caſe
of Players. "I would they would exa- Serm. ad Pop. 4. P. 252.
" mine themſelves, and their Calling, by
" this Rule. If they ſhould have been
" try'd by the Bench of Fathers and Coun-
" cils of old, or would have put it to
" moſt Voices among later Divines, both
" Popiſh and Reform'd, they had been
" utterly caſt and condem'd by the firſt
" Rule, and not have been repriev'd 'till
" now; moſt holding not the Calling on-
" ly, but the very Practice and Thing it
" ſelf unlawful and damnable. For my
" own part, I dare not at all ſay the Pra-
" ctice is, neither will I now ſay the Cal-
" ling is unlawful. Only let them that
" make a Calling of it conſider themſelves
" and their Calling well, and examine
" whether God hath not beſtow'd upon
" them ſome Gifts, which they might
" have employ'd a better way, and what
" Inducements they have, and of what
" Weight thoſe Inducements are, to give
" their Conſciences Security, that they
" have done well in embracing this as
" their Calling. And when they have thus
" done, freely and faithfully, as in the
" Sight of God, if their own Hearts con-
" demn them not, neither do I. Thus
this great and good Man declares himſelf
in Favour of Plays, and leaves the Play-

ers to be judg'd by their own Conscien-
ces: And that our Church too approves
of that his charitable Procedure, in that
Particular, is plain enough, since she neither refuses Players the Blessed Sacra-
ment, nor denies them Burial in hallow'd
Ground.

From the Councils our Author proceeds to the Fathers of the Church; who
tho' they were all Men of great Learning and exemplary Piety, were yet but
Men, and consequently not infallible.
Nay some of them, as is well known,
have held Opinions, if not downright
Heretical, yet very near approaching to
it. In particular *Tertullian,* one of those
Fathers, whom our Author represents as
the Top of their Species, held the Soul
to be immortal indeed, but then he held
it to be *Corpus effigiutum;* so that I think
'twas no such absurd or ridiculous thing
to affirm, that even the Fathers might
possibly be guilty of some Oversights,
and that through Excess of Zeal too:
Nor does it from thence follow that they
are to be read backwards, as our Author
very wittily infers, from that Mr. *Congreve's* Assertion. For my own part, I
do declare that I have as great a Veneration for those great, and good Men as
Mr. *Collier* himself can have; and shall

at

at all times submit to their Opinions, as far as any Man in Reason ought to do, that is, as far as they are either made good by Argument, or back'd by Scripture. As for a meer *ipsæ dixit*, excepting in the Case of our Blessed Saviour, who was God, or that of his Disciples, who spoke by the immediate Inspiration of the Holy Spirit, I think it less allowable in Divinity than Philosophy. But to come to the Business in hand.

I shall not in the least scruple to take all that Mr. *Collier* has presented us from the Fathers against Plays upon Content, that is, without examining how far he may have been pleas'd to clear their Sense for them. Not that I have any great Reason, considering all things, to rely on his Sincerity in that Particular, but because, after all his Address, I can find nothing that is of Weight enough to convince any one either of the Unlawfulness or Inexpediency of Plays. For all his Quotations are meerly declamatory, full of good Advice indeed, and rhetorical Flourishes against the Abuses of the Stage, but not one sound Argument, that I can meet with, against a modest and well-regulated Play. They tell us indeed, *that* View, p. *Plays were of heathen Institution, that* 253. *there was Superstition and Idolatry in the case.*

rors of Hell, or meditating on the Joys of Heaven. This, say they, is true Pleasure, this ought to be the only Employment, the only Delight of a good Christian. Very true; all this we should do, were we able; or did God require it as indispensably necessary to Salvation. But alas! we are weak and frail, and God is infinitely good and merciful. He knoweth whereof we are made, he remembreth that we are but Dust; and therefore will not require more at our Hands than we are able to perform. He does not demand every Minute of our Time, that would render not only the most innocent Diversions, but all secular and worldly Employments too criminal and sinful. *Seven times a Day do I praise thee*, says the Man after God's own Heart; and surely that Division of Time must argue an Interruption in Devotion. The Wise

Eccles. 3.4. Man tells us *there's a time for all things; a time to weep, and a time to laugh; a time to mourn, and a time to dance.* And certainly our gracious God does not only allow us the Necessaries, but the Comforts, the innocent Pleasures too of this

Eccles. 8. Life. *And then*, says the same Wise 15. Man, *I commended Mirth, because a Man hath no better thing under the Sun, than to eat, and to drink, and to be merry:*
For

*For that shall abide with him of his La-
bour, the Days of his Life, which God
giveth him under the Sun.* Length of
Days is by God himself promis'd, as a Reward of a conscionable Discharge of our
Duty to our Parents; but if all those
Days to a Minute are to be spent in Sorrow and Heaviness, Woe and Weeping
for our Sins; or in a constant Meditation
on the remoter Joys of Eternity; what
then becomes of the Temporal Blessing?
Will it not rather be a Curse? Yes surely; for if Death ought to be our only View. p. 259.
Pleasure, and to be dissolv'd and be with
Christ the only and perpetual Object of
our Desires, exclusive of all others; what
Grief, nay what Torment must it be, to
be detain'd here below, to be kept from
the Possession of those Joys we long for,
and bless'd only in a sad and tedious Con-
finement to a World of Care and Mise-
ry. I know 'tis urg'd by some, that our
Saviour himself was *a Man of Sorrow*,
and that we ought to conform our selves
so far to his Example, as to renounce all
Gaiety and worldly Pleasure. It is recorded, say they, in holy Writ, that our
Saviour wept, but we cannot find that
he ever laugh'd. But do we not read that John 2. 10.
he once honour'd a Wedding with his
Presence, a Ceremony ever attended with
Joy

Joy and Jollity; nay, was not the turning their Water into Wine, and that too after they had well drank, the very firft Miracle he ever wrought? Surely that was not done to correct but rather to encreafe their Mirth. I fhall conclude this Point, fo much (tho' againft all Reafon) infifted on, with the Opinion, or rather Advice of a Reverend and Learned Prelate of our Church, yet living, to all good Chriftians, concerning lawful Recreations and innocent Diverfions.

Parable of the Pilgrim, Cap. 22. *p.* 222. " And now I think it is time to re-
" member you, for the Prevention of all
" Miftakes, that there never was any Pil-
" grim who could always be exercis'd in
" doing good to others, or in Prayer and
" Contemplation, but he was forc'd to
" attend fometimes to himfelf alone, and
" provide for the Needs of his Body by
" the Ufe of Meat, and Drink, and Sleep;
" wherein you muft not think to be un-
" like them. Nay there is a great need
" alfo, at certain Seafons, of Innocent
" Recreations, which Pilgrims muft not
" be fo morofe as utterly to deny them-
" felves; for in truth there are none fo
" fit as they to enjoy them. And in all
" thefe things I would have you to ufe
" the beft Difcretion that is in your
" Power, avoiding, as you would the
" greateft

‘ greateſt Danger that hath been menti-
“ on’d, all fooliſhScrupuloſity about them.
“ Do not meaſure your Drink, nor weigh
“ your Meat, nor confine your Divertiſe-
“ ments to a Minute, but enjoy them
“ freely, as the beſt Wiſdom you have
“ ſhall at that preſent direct you, reſolv-
“ ing not to trouble your ſelf about any
“ after Accidents. For tho’ ’tis neceſſa-
“ ry that we take care to ſpend our Time
“ well, and there is nothing of which we
“ ſhould be more frugal; yet it is not
“ good to be over rigorous in exacting
“ an Account of our Hours. We may
“ run our ſelves thereby into infinite
“ Scruples, and buſie our Thoughts about
“ ſuch endleſs Niceties, that we may loſe
“ much Time while we are thinking how
“ to ſave it, and Impoveriſh our ſelves by
“ ſtudying to be miſerable good Huſ-
“ bands. Do not grudge therefore to
“ theſe things a fair Portion of your
“ Time, out of a fear that they will be too
“ great a Hindrance to you; for tho’
“ they ſeem to ſtay you for a while, they
“ do very much farther you, and give
“ you Strength to walk more cheerfully
“ for a long time after Diſcreet Stays
“ and Reſts make ſpeedy Journies: ’Tis
“ no turning out of your Way, to divert
“ your ſelf ſome time in a pleaſant Mea-

L   “dow.

" dow. That is the neareſt Way to a
" Place which brings you ſooneſt thither;
" and as the old Saying is, *Soft and Fair*
" *goes far*.

But what then! Do the Fathers endeavour to impoſe upon us, whilſt they
ſo earneſtly diſſuade us from all Pleaſures
and Diverſions, in particular that of the
Stage? Or is it poſſible that Plays ſhould
be now lawful, which thoſe good and pious
Men declaim'd againſt with ſo much Zeal
and Rhetorick? Yes it is; not only poſſible but very probable, and all, even
their ſevereſt Expreſſions againſt them,
will be, if not entirely juſtify'd, yet in a
great meaſure excus'd, and the Stage for
all that ſtand fair enough, in the Opinion of all reaſonable and unprejudic'd Perſons, if we conſider,

Firſt, The Perſons that wrote.
Secondly, The Time they wrote in. And,
Thirdly, The Nature of thoſe Plays
    they wrote againſt.

And Firſt for the Perſons that wrote.
They were all Men of great Learning and
extraordinary Sanctity, Men that willingly paſs'd through the greateſt Severi-
ties of a Monaſtick Life, and renounc'd
not only the Joys, the Pleaſures, but in

a great meafure the Bufinefs too of the World. Men, on whom God Almighty, in Favour, in Pity and Compaffion of his diftrefs'd Church, pour'd down more than ordinary Bleffings, and a larger Portion of his Grace: Men, in fhort, that by a long and affiduous Study, and conftant Practice of Piety, defervedly rais'd themfelves above the common Level of Mankind, and have ever fince been honour'd and diftinguifh'd by all fucceeding Ages as the Fathers of the Church: And what wonder now, if thefe good and pious Men, who had themfelves attain'd to fo great a Perfection of Piety, fhould zealoufly Exhort and vigoroufly Provoke others to the like? What wonder, I fay, that they who had not only renounc'd the Pomps and Vanities, but even the moft innocent Pleafures of the World, fhould with fome Warmth endeavour to diffuade others from them? Befides, they very well knew, that Men are by Nature but too much addicted to Pleafure, and apt enough of themfelves, without any other Encouragement, to lay hold on all thofe Privileges the Chriftian Religion could allow; and therefore perhaps they did not think it advifable to amufe themfelves in fhewing juft how far People in that Cafe might venture without danger

L 2   of

of being loft, but rather chofe to urge
them ftill on, in that which they con-
ceiv'd the directeft way to Heaven. All
Pleafures, all manner of Diverfions they
run down as dangerous and bewitching
Snares; nor would they allow of one
fingle Thought but what mounted up-
wards: A Piece of Severity which in
thefe our Times would certainly do more
hurt than good, and make perhaps fome
Atheifts, a great many Hypocrites, but
very few Saints; yet then it was feafo-
nable, then 'twas in a manner neceffary,
and therefore will appear yet more ex-
cufable in thofe good Fathers, if, in the
next place, we confider

The Time they wrote in. Now moft
of the Fathers quoted by Mr. *Collier* liv'd
in the Second or Third Century, fome in
the Fourth; and all, fays he, fall within the
Compafs of the Fifth; and he values himfelf ftrangely upon it, with what Reafon
we fhall fee prefently. The Chriftian, for
the firft three hundred Years after our
Saviour, was grievoufly opprefs'd, and
under a perpetual Cloud; all its Profef-
fors were either perfecuted in a moft
cruel and bloody manner by the Emperors, or elfe continually harrafs'd, wrong'd
and abus'd, revil'd, flander'd and infult-
ed by their Heathen Neighbours: All
                                                their

their beſt Actions were ſhamefully tra-
duc'd, and their very Devotions repreſented as Criminal. In a Word, they
were ſlighted, they were deſpis'd, they
were hated on all Hands; and as a Flock
of harmleſs Sheep plac'd in the midſt of
ravening Wolves, they were ſurrounded
by Heathens, and encompaſs'd by Blaſ-
phemers; they were aſſaulted on all Sides,
and every Minute ready to be devour'd
by thoſe bitter and implacable Enemies
of the Croſs. And was that time of Per-
ſecution and Oppreſſion a time for Pleaſure, a time for Plays? No certainly, no
Pleaſures, no Diverſions could then be
Innocent; and therefore no wonder if the
Fathers declaim'd ſo violently againſt all.
Thoſe poor Chriſtians had certainly
enough to do to defend themſelves and
their Religion againſt the bare-fac'd, open
and eager Oppoſition of the whole World,
and the more ſecret and almoſt impercep-
tible Machinations of the Devil; who
then, no doubt of it, redoubled his In-
duſtry, and with all his Might, all his
Malice, endeavour'd to obſtruct the
Growth of a Religion he hated. But
now, thanks be to our good and gracious God, the Affairs of Religion are in
a much better Poſture, the State now
countenances, protects and cheriſhes the

L 3   Church.

Church. And whereas Labour and Sorrow, Care and Poverty, were, for the first three hundred Years after Christ, the constant Attendants of all those who waited at the Altar; now Wealth and Honour, Ease and Plenty, are the just Rewards of that Service; and our Modern Clergy are not only cloath'd with Righteousness, but do sing with Joyfulness. And when the Shepherds rejoice should the Sheep mourn? Shall not we too reap all the Benefits of this blessed Calm, and be put in Possession of all those Privileges our holy Religion can indulge? Certainly whatever those good Fathers might say in those times of Trouble and Distraction, we may now safely enough pretend to several innocent Liberties, several harmless Diversions, as Refreshments to our wearied Bodies and drooping Spirits, which they might not then think allowable. For Mr. *Collier* imposes upon us strangely, when he would make us believe, that the very Time of their Writing is an Argument against Plays. For tho', in Matters of Doctrine, the concurring Opinions of those Fathers which liv'd nearest to our Saviour's time, are, and ought to be, of greatest Weight and Authority with us; yet in Matters meerly indifferent the Case is otherwise, and

and differing Circumstances may and will justifie a quite different Conduct in Church as well as State. What I have said of the three first, will in a great measure hold good of the two succeeding Centuries: For tho' the Christian Religion was first establish'd, and openly own'd and protected in the Empire by *Constantine,* yet was not the Heathen Superstition totally abolish'd in a long time after, but continu'd, even in *Rome* it self, 'till the time of the Emperor *Theodosius,* by whom it was at last utterly suppress'd. But the Christians were no sooner freed from their fears of the Heathens, when the *Arian* Heresie gave Birth to new Troubles, new Distractions in the Church; and almost as fierce Persecutions against all Orthodox Christians as ever they had suffer'd from the Heathen. To conclude this Point, the Time in which those Fathers wrote, might be a good Argument against the Use of Plays then, but can conclude nothing either against the Lawfulness or Expediency of them now, and their great Severity against that Diversion in particular, may be yet better accounted for, and that without any Reflection on our Modern Stage, under a due Regulation, if, in the last Place, we consider

The

The Nature of thofe Plays they wrote againft.

And here, how much foever fome People may pretend to be in the Dark as to this Matter, yet the Fathers themfelves give us fome, and the very Times more Light into the Nature of thofe Plays they wrote againft. That they were extreamly Lewd we may conclude from the Fathers; and that they were both Superftitious and Idolatrous we may well believe when we confider, that for a long time after our Saviour, both Poets and Players were certainly Heathen; and therefore in all probability they never writ nor acted Plays without fome regard had to the Reafon of their Original Inftitution. Nor was that perhaps the worft of the Bufinefs neither; the Primitive Chriftians we all know, were in thofe times of Darknefs defpis'd, laugh'd at and affronted by every one, and can we then think a Heathen Stage fhould fpare them? Is it not rather probable that the Poets of thofe times might not only ridicule them, but expofe their Faith too, and make merry with the moft facred Myfteries of their Religion? This, tho' not certain, is at leaft extreamly probable; and when the Fathers tax thofe Chriftians that frequented the Play-houfe, as herding with

Blaf-

Blafphemers; I cannot but think they hint at fome fuch hellifh Practice, which yet they could not enlarge upon without Horror. And if the Cafe were fo, no body, I think, can blame the Fathers for the great Bitternefs of their Invectives againft the Stage then, or think they any way concern Plays now, at leaft as they may and ought to be Reform'd. And fo having done with the Fathers, I dare appeal to the equal Judgment of any impartial Reader, whether Mr. *Collier* has fo much Reafon to triumph, as he pretends to on their Occafion? 'Tis true, he tells us, that he has given us the Opinion of the Church for the firft five hundred Years, and that fhe has cenfur'd the Stage both in Councils and fingle Authorities; and indeed I am fo far of his Mind, that fhe has done it in both alike, that is in neither. For her Councils condemn Players but not Plays, the Calling, but not the Thing; and her Fathers declaim only againft the Abufes of the Stage, or if by chance there be any thing of Argument to be met with againft Plays in general, mingled with their Satyr againft thofe of their own Times, 'twill conclude ev'ry whit as fully againft all manner of Diverfions how innocent foever, as againft that of Plays. I fhall there-

therefore paſs by his Sophiſtical Harrangue on the Fathers, and the Time
they writ in, and come to his Conclu-
ſion.

And here now, I ſhould have thought,
he would have ſum'd up his Evidence,
and demanded Judgment againſt the
Stage. But he cares not to give over ſo,
he has ſtill new Matter to object, he has
ſtill an aching Tooth not only at all Poets,
Plays and Players, but at all others any
way belonging to them; and now therefore he falls foul on the Fidlers. Their
Muſick, he ſays, is dangerous, and tho'
in truth it utters neither Bawdy, Blaſphemy or Atheiſm, yet is it, if you will believe him, an admirable Vehicle to convey
them all into the Heart, Blood and Guts
of an Audience. But, I muſt confeſs,
I have not the Patience to trace him any
farther on this Subject, his Notions are
all ſo very whimſical, extravagant and
conceited, that I cannot but think the
beſt Anſwer they deſerve to be a Smile.

Our Author, having taken his full Swing,
by way of Harrangue, againſt the Play-
houſe Muſick, tells us there are yet two
things behind, which would ſtick upon
the Stage, and have an ill Effect upon the
Audience. The firſt of which is their
dilating ſo much upon the Argument of
Love.

Love. I could wish he would tell us what
sort of Love he means; if honest, if honourable Love, I leave it then to himself
to consider, whether he be not fallen into the same Fault which he so often con-
demns in our Plays. For certainly he
that speaks slightly of such Love, and
tells us that the treating of that Subject
home, is but a cunning way of stealing
upon the blind Side, and practising on
the Weakness of Human Nature; not only discourages, but speaks as scandalously
and as maliciously against Matrimony, as
any of our Stage-Poets can do. But let
that pass, and let him say what he will,
and mean what he pleases, Love, tho'
not altogether Innocent, may be innocently enough manag'd on the Stage, and
that too without raising such a Tumult
of Passions in the Audience as he dreams
of. This is a truth so evident, that I shall
not trouble my self to prove it, but only
give my Reader the Opinion of the famous *Boileau* on the Case, and so leave
it.

Je ne suis pas pourtant de ces tristes,
　　　　　　　　　　　(esprits,
Qui bannissant l'amour de tous chastes
　　　　　　　　　　　(écrits,

L'Art.
Poetique
Chant.
p. 216. 4.

D'unsi

D'unfi riche ornement veulent priver
                                    (la scene:
Traitent d'empoisenneurs & Roderique
                                    (& Chimene
L'amour le moins honeste, exprimé cha-
                                    (stement,
N'excite point en nous de honteux mo-
                                    (vement;
Didon a beau gemir, & m'etaler ses
                                    (charmes,
Je condamne sa faute, en partageant
                                    (ses larmes.

The next thing he objects against the
Stage is their encouraging Revenge. *What
is more common*, says he, *than Duels and
Quarrellings in their Characters of Figure?* He confesses indeed, that this de-
sperate Custom is no Original of the Stage;
but then he is very angry that they do
not check the Growth of it; by which
we may guess, that for all his Flourishes,
Plays, did the Poets so please, might be
good for something. But in this Particular, I must needs say he's unreasonable,
and too hard in all Conscience upon those
Gentlemen, to expect that they should
put a stop to that prevailing Folly in our
Men of Honour, which even his own
dear Moral Essays have not been hitherto
able to prevent. To draw towards an
End.   Tho'

View, p. 283.

Tho' Mr. *Collier,* in the Beginning of this Chapter, declares against all Plays, without Exception, as Nurseries of Vice, and Corrupters of Youth; from whence we may reasonably enough infer, that he holds them unlawful too; yet no where, in his *View* at least, has he in plain Terms confess'd so much. He very frequently indeed speaks plainly enough to be understood, but no where so plain as to be convicted of a direct Design against the Stage. I shall not trouble my self to enquire into the Reason of this Piece of Policy of his, but that he may not make any great Advantage of it, I shall here take Occasion to shew the Reader, what he would at last have him believe to be his real Opinion concerning Plays. *I affirm,* says he, *that Plays are plainly condemn'd in Scripture upon two Accounts.* First upon the Score of Idolatry, as they were a Part of Pagan Worship. But that Reason expiring with the Heathen Religion, he insists not on it. But then, Secondly, he says, the Stage (particularly the *English* one) is condemn'd in Scripture upon the Score of Smut and Prophaness, upon the Account of the Danger and Indecencies of such Liberties: And why now is that Parenthesis thrust in, what has he here to do either with the

Reply to the Relap. *p.* 133.

the *English,* or any other particular Stage, where the thing he himself propoſes to prove, is that all Plays in general are condemn'd in Scripture? But there's Art in Dawbing, and this little innocent Parentheſis may ſtand as a remarkable Inſtance of Mr. *Collier's* Addreſs in the Management of a weak Cauſe. For he very well knowing, that none of his Scripture Proofs could come up to his firſt Pretenſions againſt all Plays, was willing to lay ſomething in the way that they might take hold of: Not doubting, I ſuppoſe, but that his kind, candid, godly Reader, would ſwallow the Wrong, and wink at the Change that was put upon him, provided he did but maul the *English* Stage to ſome purpoſe: And therein his Hopes have not been altogether diſappointed. But let that paſs; and let us now conſider his Proofs from Scripture, and ſee how far they will affect all Plays.

Mat. 5. 34.   St. *Matthew* tells us we muſt *not Swear at all*: And yet Swearing in ſeveral Cauſes, is not only lawful, but neceſſary.
Ephes. 5.4.   St. *Paul* tells us we are to *put away all*
Colloſſ. 3.8. *Blaſphemy and filthy Communication out of our Mouth:* To theſe Texts I have ſpoken in another Place, and therefore ſhall ſay no more here, but that there are and may be many Plays without any thing of either.   St. *Pe-*

St. *Peter* tells us we must *serve God with Reverence*, we must *be Sober and Vigilant* : Are all innocent and harmless Diversions inconsistent with the Service of God? Or because we must be Sober, must we never be Chearful? And because we are to be Vigilant, must we never Sleep? ^{1 Pet: 5. 8.}

The same St. *Peter* tell us, that we must *pass the time of our Sojourning here in Fear* : Very true; in an awful and reverend Fear of God, but not in such a perpetual, slavish Fear, as shall sour all the innocent Enjoyments of this World. ^{1 Peter 1. 17.}

St. *Paul* again bids us *abstain from all Appearance of Evil*: Right; but then we ought to be convinc'd of that Appearance of Evil from which we are oblig'd to abstain: We are not bound to take Mr. *Collier*'s Word, in the Case, that I know of. ^{1 Thes. 5. 22.}

To conclude; the same St. *Paul* tells us, we are to take no Pleasure in scandalous Practices, and *have no Fellowship with the unfruitful Works of Darkness*: When Mr. *Collier*, or any one else for him, has fairly proved all Plays to be such, we will have done with them. ^{Rom. 1. 32. Ephes. 5. 11.}

And now what can all these Texts of Scripture, which he has rally'd against the Stage, and which condemn only the

the Abuses of it, signifie against Plays in general? Yet our Author, as if he had made good all his Pretensions to a Tittle, begins to swell, and look big upon his Performance. *Here,* says he, *is Evidence enough in all Reason:* What, against all Plays? no, no; that is but an impertinent Question in this Place. *These Admonitions,* says he, *are full against our Stage.* The wonderful Confidence of some Men! He first pretends to prove all Plays condemn'd in Scripture, and in Order to it produces a great many Texts, and then at last concludes, that all those Texts are full against our *English* Stage. Again he tells us, *that not one Play in forty can stand the Test of so much as one single Text.* But does he mean this of our Plays in particular, or of all Plays? For my part I know not where to have him: And yet let him mean what he will, I dare boldly affirm that there are many such good and modest Plays frequently Acted, even on our Stage, as upon the Test might stand against every one of those Texts he has quoted. And therefore, tho' some few of our Plays are plainly enough censur'd by them; yet can it not be properly said, that our *English* Stage stands condemn'd by Scripture; unless Mr. *Collier* will pretend to prove,

that

[margin note: Reply to the Relap. p. 134.]

[margin note: Ibid.]

that we neither have, nor can have any
Plays, but what are, and muſt be ſtuff'd
with Bawdy, Blaſphemy, or Atheiſm.

But our Author, ſenſible no doubt of
his own Failings, calls in the Biſhop of
Meaux to his Aſſiſtance; tho' not ſo
much, I believe, to help him, as to keep him
in Countenance. For to ſpeak the plain
Truth, the Biſhop mends the Matter but
very little. 'Tis true, he pretends to argue againſt the Stage, and that from
Scripture too; but then he either wreſts
it to a wrong Senſe, or infers more from
it than the Text will bear. He either
runs upon a falſe Suppoſition of the Ne-
ceſſity of a conſtant and uninterrupted
Devotion, which can never be prov'd;
or pretends that we cannot make uſe of
any, the moſt innocent Diverſions of
this World, without contracting ſuch a
Habit of Pleaſure, as muſt be ſinful. I
ſhall therefore paſs by his Arguments of
Weak and Vicious, and only ſtop a
little to conſider his Harangue; which,
in my Opinion, is very remarkable. For
all on a ſudden the good Biſhop grows
ſtrangely fond of the *Jews*, that faithleſs
and ſtubborn Generation, and becauſe Pſalm 78.
forſooth they had no Plays amongſt them, 9.
he winks at their Idolatry, overlooks
their frequent Rebellions againſt the Al-
M   mighty,

mighty, and quite forgetting how they
Pſalm 78. griev'd God with their Hill-Altars, and
59. provok'd him to Diſpleaſure with their
Images; he tells us " They had no Shews
" to entertain them but their Feaſts, their
" Sacrifices, and their holy Ceremonies.
" They were form'd, ſays he, by their
" Conſtitution to a plain, and natural
" Way of living: They knew nothing of
" theſe Fancies, and Inventions of *Greece*;
" ſo that to the Praiſes that *Balaam* gives
" them, That there's no Inchantment in
" *Jacob*, nor Divination in *Iſrael*, we
" may likewiſe add, there was no Thea-
" ter among them, nothing of theſe dan-
" gerous Amuſements to be met with:
" This innocent and undebauch'd People
" took their Recreations at home, and
" made their Children their Diverſion:
That is, if you will believe the Royal
Pſalmiſt, they offer'd their Sons and their
Pſalm 181. Daughters unto Devils, to the Idols of
16, 17. *Canaan*. And indeed to this innocent
and undebauch'd People it was, that
God himſelf ſpake by the Prophet *Jere-*
miah, ſaying, *How ſhall I pardon thee for*
Jer. 5. 7, 8. *this? Thy Children have forſaken me, and*
ſworn by them that are no Gods; when
I had fed them to the full, then they com-
mitted Adultery, and aſſembled themſelves
by Troops in the Harlots Houſes. They

were

*were as fed Horses in the Morning, every
one neighed after his Neighbour's Wife.*
And to the same innocent and undebauch'd
People it was, that the Prophet *Hosea*
spake, saying, *Hear the Word of the Lord* Hosea 4. 1.
ye Children of Israel, *for the Lord hath a* 2.
*Controversie with the Inhabitants of the
Land, because there is no Truth, nor Mercy, nor Knowledge of God in the Land.
By swearing, and lying, and killing, and
stealing, and committing Adultery, they
break out, and Blood toucheth Blood.* Thus
unless we'll rather believe the Bishop of
Meaux, than those Holy Men the Pro-
phets we may plainly enough perceive
what were the most usual Diversions of
that innocent and undebauch'd People
that had no Plays amongst them.

And so I shall leave this Bishop, and
his extravagant and fulsome Flourish on
the *Jews :* By which however we may
plainly see, into what strange and ridiculous Absurdities the most ingenious of
Men are apt to fall; who, when once
engag'd in a bad Cause, for want of Arguments are forc'd to rely on their Wit ;
and when they cannot fairly convince,
must needs endeavour to impose upon
their Readers. And indeed by these, and
such like Arts as these, this Controversie
concerning Plays has been always main-

tain'd,

tain'd, and is still kept on foot. Mr. *Collier's View* is an undeniable Instance of that sort of Management now in these our Times, and the learned Bishop *Sanderson* will tell us how this, and some other Disputes of the like, tho' indeed of a much higher Nature, were carry'd on in his. " I dare say, says that great Man,

Serm. ad Aula 11. p. 224.

" whosoever shall peruse with a judicious
" and impartial Eye most of those Pam-
" phlets that in this daring Age have
" been thrust into the World, against the
" Ceremonies of the Church, against E-
" piscopal Government, (to pass by things
" of lesser Regard and Usefulness, and
" more open to Exception and Abuse,
" yet, so far as I can understand, unjust-
" ly condemn'd as things utterly unlaw-
" ful; such as are lusorious Lots, Dan-
" cing, Stage-Plays, and some other
" things of like nature) when he shall
" have drain'd out the bitter Invectives,
" unmannerly Jeers, petulant girding at
" those that are in Authority, imperti-
" nent Digressions, but above all those
" most bold and perverse Wrestings of
" Holy Scripture, wherewith such Books
" are infinitely stuff'd; he shall find that
" little poor Remainder that is left be-
" hind to contain but κενὲς λόγες, vain
" Words and empty Arguments. For
" when

" when these great Undertakers have
" snatch'd up the Bucklers, as if they
" would make it good against all Comers,
" that such and such things are utterly
" unlawful, and therefore ought in all
" Reason and Conscience to bring such
" Proofs as will come up to that Con-
" clusion; *Quid dignum tanto?* Very sel-
" dom shall you hear from them any o-
" ther Arguments than such as will con-
" clude an Inexpediency at most: As that
" they are apt to give Scandal, that they
" carry with them an Appearance of E-
" vil, that they are often Occasions of
" Sin, that they are not commanded in
" the Word, and such like.   Which Ob-
" jections, even where they are just, are
" not of Force (no, not taken all toge-
" ther, much less any of them singly) to
" prove a thing to be utterly unlawful.
" And yet are they glad many times, ra-
" ther than sit out, to play very small
" Game, and to make use of Arguments
" yet weaker than these, and such as will
" not reach so far as to prove a bare In-
" expediency: As that they were invent-
" ed by Heathens, that they have been
" abus'd in Popery, and other such like.
" Which, to my Understanding, is a ve-
" ry strong Presumption that they have
" taken a very weak Cause in hand, and
                              " such

" such as is wholly destitute of sound
" Proof: For if they had any better Ar-
" guments, think ye we should not hear
" of them? Thus far the Bishop. And
now I shall not trouble my self to shew,
how far either the Malice or the Weakness of our Author's Arguments against
Plays may have expos'd him to the same
Censure, which this good and pious Man
has here pass'd on the Pamphleteers of
the last Age. I very willingly wave the
enlarging on so ungrateful a Subject. One
thing however I must observe, and that is
this, That whereas this Reverend and
Learned Prelate very well understood the
utmost Force of all Mr. *Collier*'s Authorities, whether Heathen or Christian,
tho' he were well read in the Councils,
and throughly conversant in all the Works
of the Fathers of the Church, yet he
here declares plainly in Favour of Plays:
This Bishop, I say, who for Piety, Learning, and a most profound Judgment, was
equal to any one of the Fathers, and
whose Authority, in this present Dispute
about Plays at least, ought to weigh more
with us than all theirs put together: Because we certainly know the Nature of
those Plays, of which he here delivers
his Opinion; but can only guess what
they

they might be, againſt which the Fathers let fly ſo many bitter Invectives.

To conclude; I think I may now ſafely ſay, that I have made good my firſt Pretenſions againſt Mr. *Collier;* for certainly he can be no fair Reformer, that endeavours the Deſtruction of the thing to be Reform'd; as by ſeveral Inſtances I have plainly made it appear he has done. And when he pretends to pull off his Mask, and ſhew himſelf an Enemy, I hope I have ſo anſwer'd all his moſt material Objections, and given ſo fair and probable an Account of thoſe many Authorities he has rally'd againſt the Stage, as may ſufficiently vindicate the Innocency of all well regulated Plays, and in ſome meaſure abate the Pride of an Adverſary, but too long accuſtom'd to triumph.

F I N I S.